CHANNEL ISLANDS' MILITARY HERITAGE

ANDREW POWELL-THOMAS

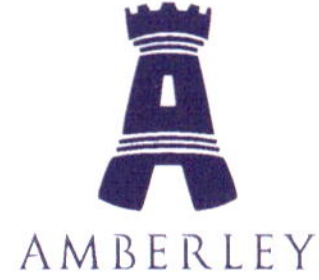

First published 2024

Amberley Publishing
The Hill, Stroud,
Gloucestershire, GL5 4EP

www.amberley-books.com

ISBN: 978 1 3981 1283 4 (print)
ISBN: 978 1 3981 1284 1 (ebook)

British Library Cataloguing in Publication Data.
A catalogue record for this book is available from the British Library.

Typeset in 10pt on 13pt Celeste.
Origination by Amberley Publishing.
Printed in the UK.

Contents

Introduction

The Channel Islands sit nestled in the English Channel just a few miles west of the Cotentin peninsula of France. Over 170,000 people call these numerous islands home, inhabiting seven of them, and they understandably mix the very best of British and French cultures. Their sheltered position in the Bay of St Malo means that it is generally warmer and has more sunshine hours than you would get on mainland Britain, and the islands are renowned for their extraordinary variety of landscapes. However, due to their geographic location it isn't surprising that they have a long and somewhat staggering military heritage. Being crown dependencies, over the centuries the locals have formed militias to help protect and defend the islands, whilst also accommodating British troops in grand castles and impressive forts, fending off invading French attacks over the centuries. Of course, the German occupation during the Second World War has left a more recent and permanent mark on the island, with bunkers, command posts and workers' camps still visible amongst the landscape today.

Chapter 1

Jersey

Archirondel Tower

Jutting out from the middle of St Catherine's Bay, on an offshore rocky outcrop called La Roche Rondel, is Archirondel Tower. Taking two years to construct, it was completed in 1794 as tower number 22 of 30 planned around the Island by General Conway in order to deter a potential French invasion. Garrisoned with soldiers of the Artillery and Engineers, it was soon decided to add to the position by building a permanent gun platform around

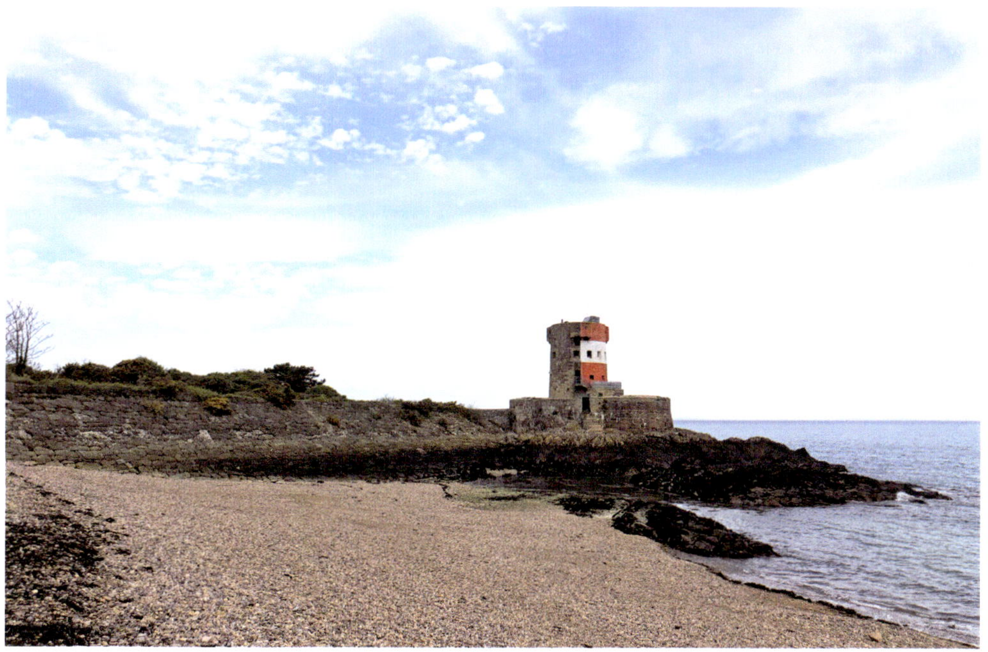

Archirondel Tower is built on the small *La Roche Rondel* – originally a tidal island before it was connected by a causeway. (Author's collection)

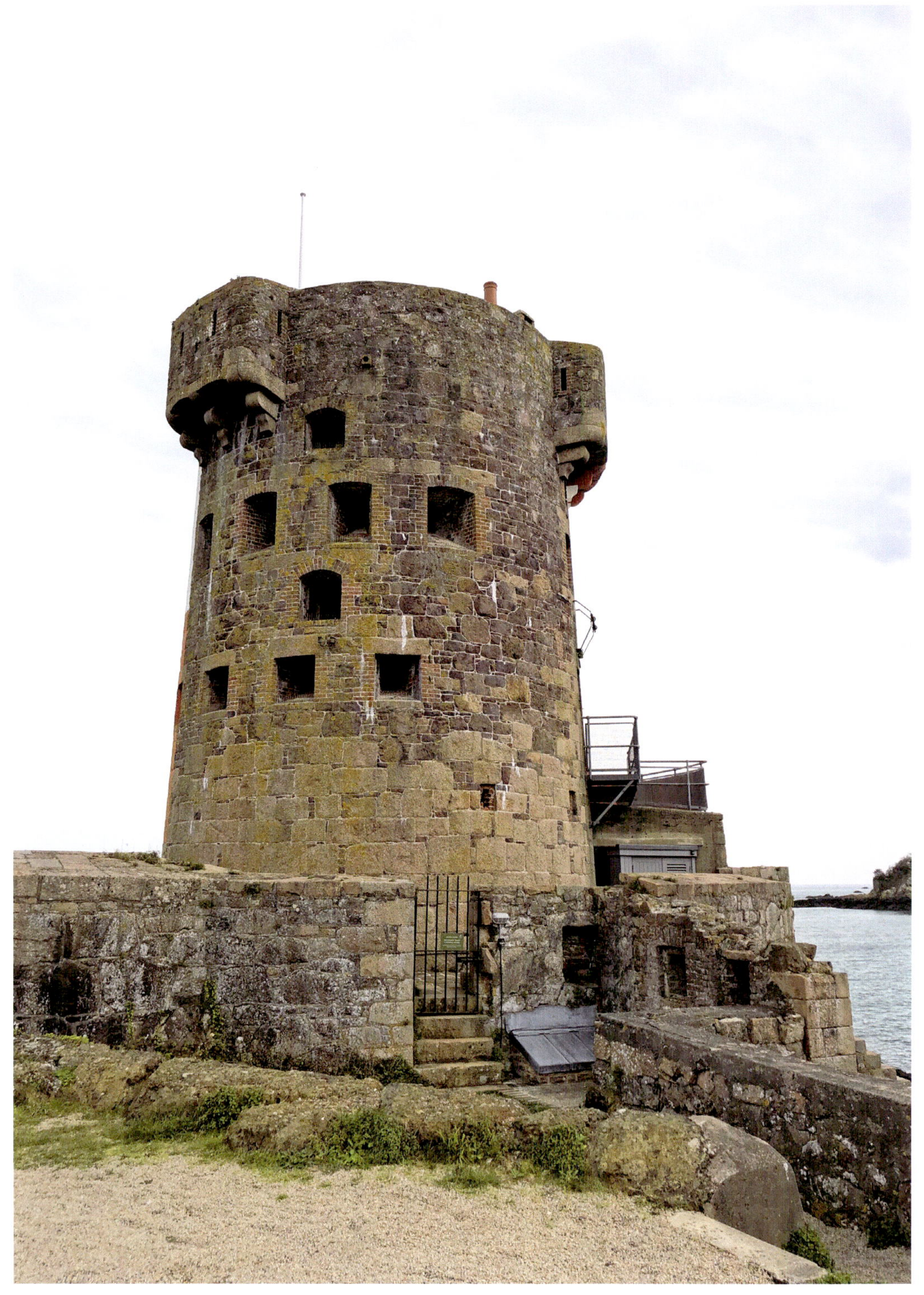

Archirondel Tower is one of twenty-two towers built on the island by the former Governor of Jersey, Field Marshall Henry Conway. (Author's collection)

the base of the tower. The tower remained an important part of Jersey's defensive works, and it was garrisoned and operational until the 1860s, when it became redundant. In 1923, the tower was purchased from the Crown by the States of Jersey, although it still remained unused and obsolete. However, in the Second World War, German Occupying Forces saw an opportunity to use this already standing defensive position for themselves. The floors were replaced with concrete, a new entrance was created at ground level, along with a small extension for machine guns to be mounted, and the position was manned throughout the occupation. After the war it remained closed, but in 2006 it became registered as owned by the Public of the Island of Jersey, and since 2019, Jersey Heritage have overseen a refit and modernisation of its interior, to enable the tower to be let out as a rather spectacular self-catering property.

Batterie Lothringen

The German occupation of Jersey during the Second World War has understandably left its mark on the island. Hitler's plans for Jersey included constructing nine coastal batteries that would cover the gulf of St Malo and offer protection to German shipping between the strategic ports of Brest and Cherbourg on mainland France. Batterie Lothringen was one of these. The location of Noirmont Point was an obvious place to put a defensive coastal battery, jutting out as it does from the south coast of Jersey and offering significant protection to the port of St Helier – although its traversable guns were, in theory, able to attack targets approaching the island from any direction. Construction started in the spring of 1941 with three old 15 cm naval guns from the First World War being installed as a temporary measure whilst work took place on the more permanent concrete positions of the site. These positions were built with the intention of receiving more modern quick-firing turreted naval guns, but the Allied bombing of factories and production lines in Germany meant that the temporary older guns actually became the permanent feature. As with all large coastal batteries the site was defended by a number of additional installations and Lothringen had six anti-aircraft guns, two heavy machine gun nests, sixteen flamethrower positions, eleven gun emplacements, two mortars and one anti-tank gun! A static 60 cm searchlight and a railed 110 cm searchlight were positioned here – not to mention numerous ammunition bunkers, metre upon metre of barbed wire and minefields. It was a huge battery. The temporary command post that was built in 1941 was replaced in 1944 with a bigger and stronger command post on the most southerly point of the battery and looks very much like the bridge of a battleship. This two-storey command post, the nerve centre of the site, took a year to construct (March 1943–April 1944) and is predominately underground – with only the 6-metre range-finder turret being above ground. The command bunker had twenty-five men on duty at all times, with accommodation, central heating, air conditioning, toilets and showers built within its depths.

Manned by over 170 men of Naval Artillery Battalion 604, Lothringen was the third battery under their control, with the other two on Guernsey and Alderney respectively. Although there were wooden barrack huts on site, the vast majority of the men were actually billeted at the (former) Portelet Holiday Camp! Aside from live firing drills, the guns at Lothringen were only fired in anger a few times. In December 1942, its weapons brought down two RAF aircraft that were attacking a German convoy, but the allies mainly steered clear of the area. In the months after D-Day there was an understandable increase in activity, but by September 1944, when the Allies had liberated the nearby French coastline, they were simply able to avoid Lothringen's guns – making them just an interested spectator to the ongoing liberation of Europe.

When the Channel Islands were finally liberated in May 1945, the large guns were dumped over the cliffs at Les Landes in the north-west of the island, and anything that could be taken from the bunkers was. The Noirmont headland was purchased by the States of Jersey in January 1947 for the public as the island's war memorial and the various bunkers were sealed up in 1948. They lay there abandoned for over thirty years, until the Channel Islands Occupation Society (CIOS) obtained permission to restore the command bunker and observation tower because of the historical significance of the site – and what a job they have done! Although the external parts of Lothringen are available to see all year round, it is worth keeping an eye out for the days, and there are always a number of these across the year, when the CIOS open up the command bunker. It is staggering. Also part of the Noirmont Point site, although not open to the public, is the impressive MP1 Naval Direction and Range-Finding Tower. Standing at over 15 metres tall, it was built down into the cliff and is unique on the island as its entrance is on the top floor!

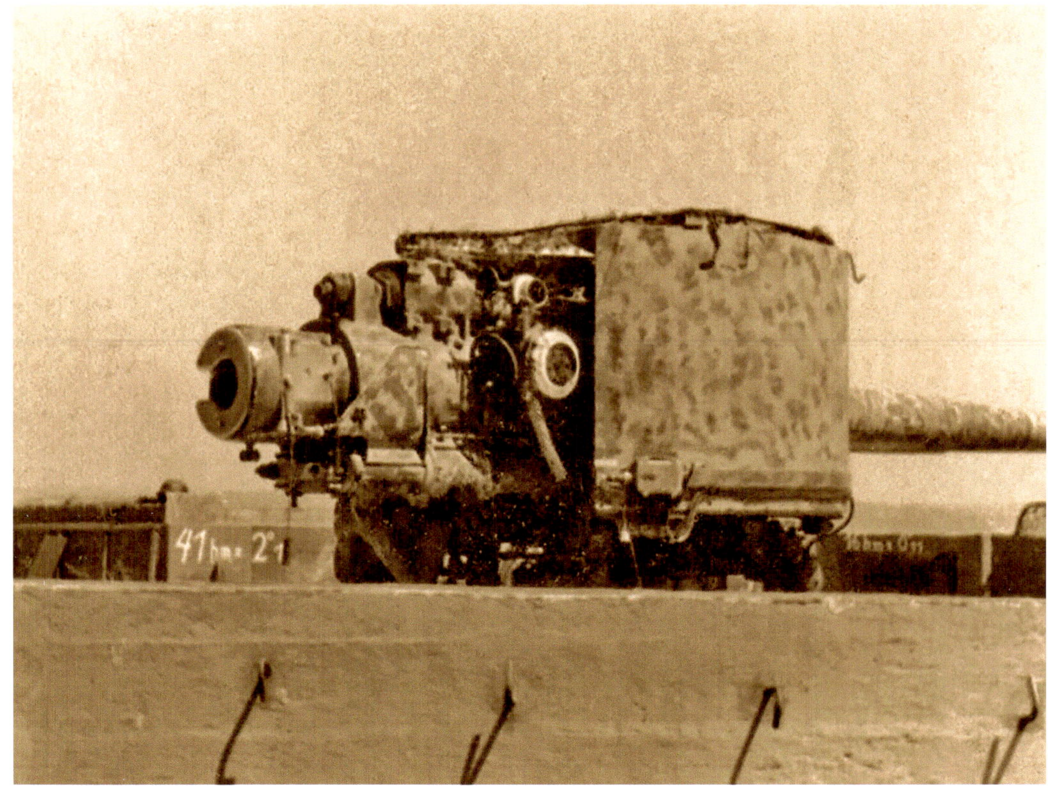

A view of No. 1 Gun position during the occupation. (Courtesy of the Channel Island Occupation Society (Jersey))

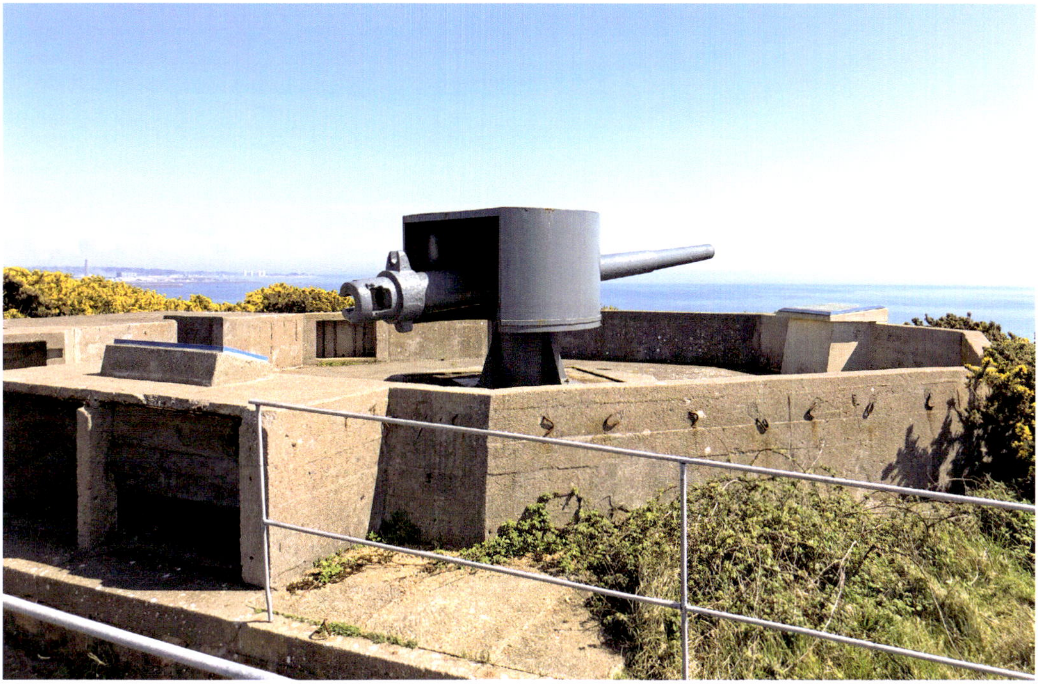

No. 1 Gun position today. (Author's collection)

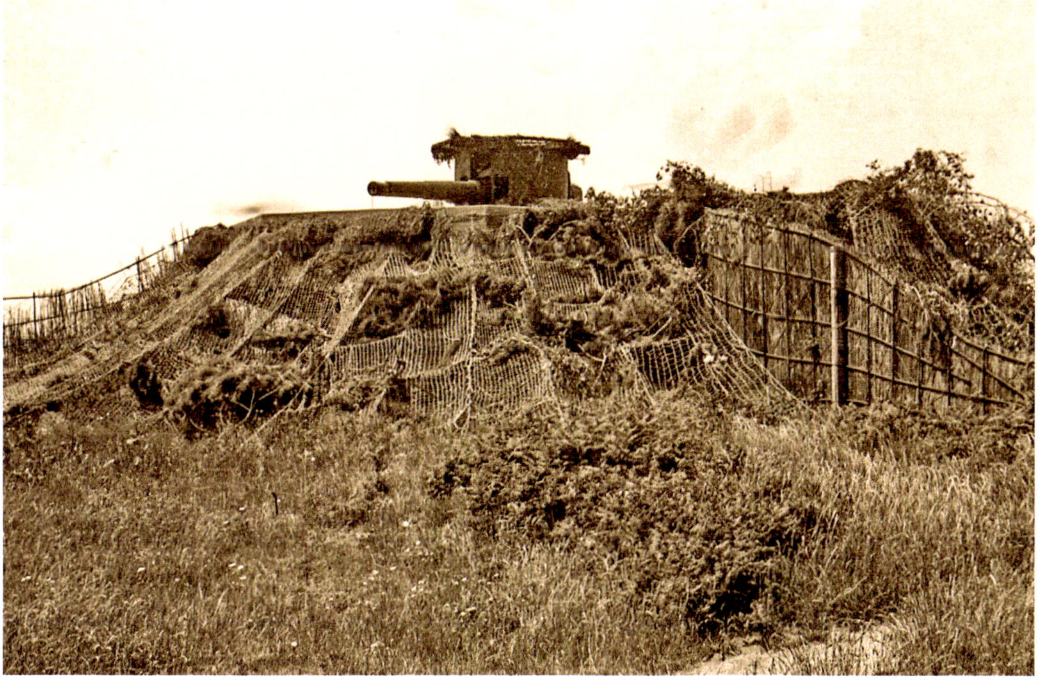

Batterie Lothringen during the Second World War – note the camouflage netting! (Courtesy of the Channel Island Occupation Society (Jersey)/Jersey Evening Post)

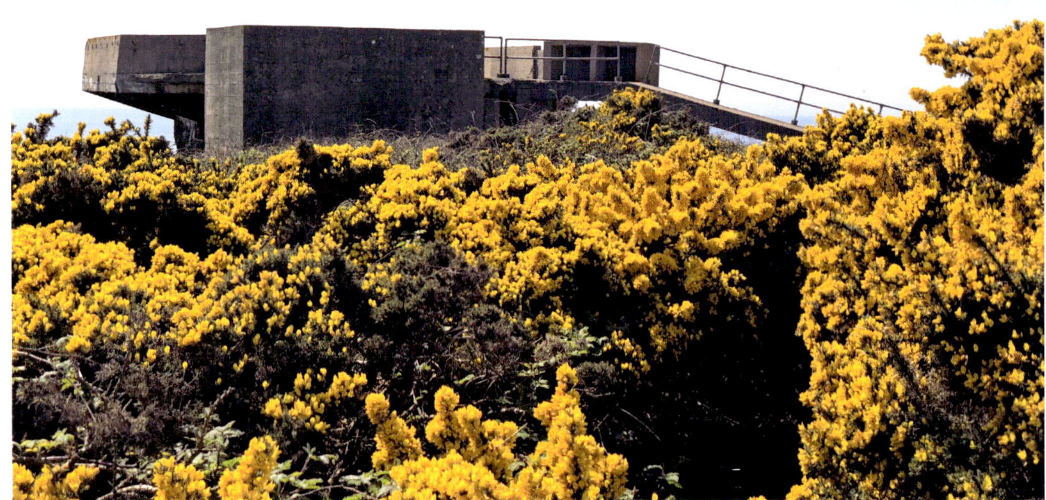

The same position today – No. 4 Gun is now surrounded by the vegetation on Noirmant Point. (Author's collection)

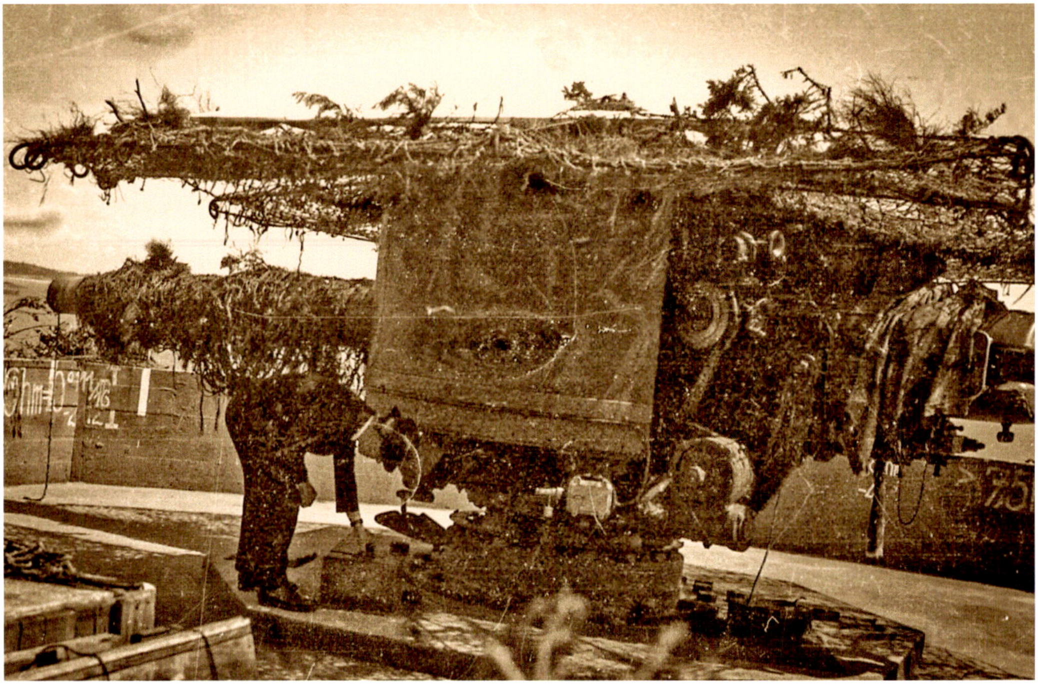

A close-up of one of the camouflaged 6.5-ton gun barrels during the conflict. (Courtesy of the Channel Island Occupation Society (Jersey))

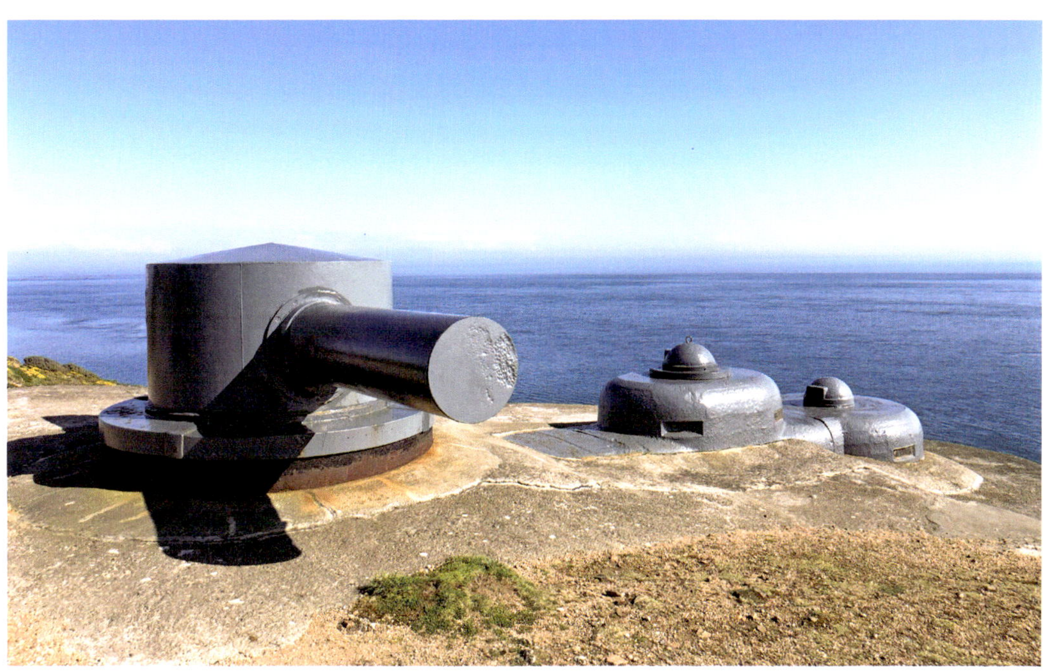

The visible part of the command bunker, or *Leitstand*, above ground looks like the bridge of a battleship. To the left is the armoured range-finder turret. (Author's collection)

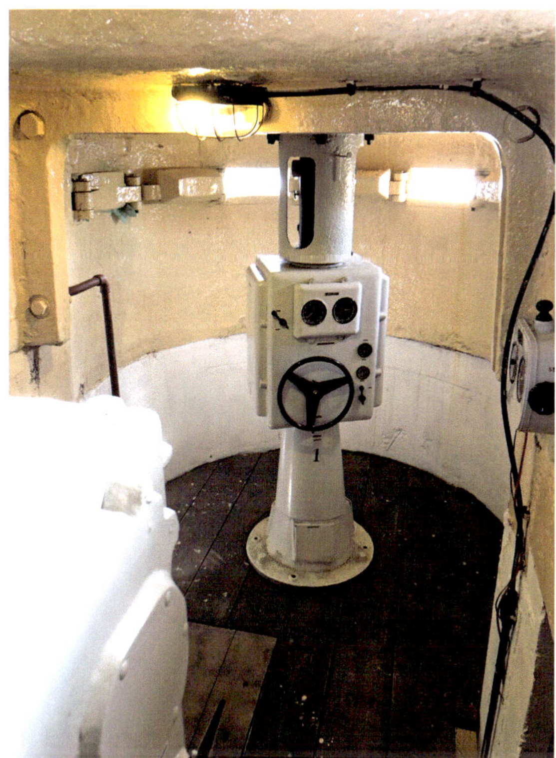

One of the azimuth periscopes used to determine the direction of a target. (Author's collection)

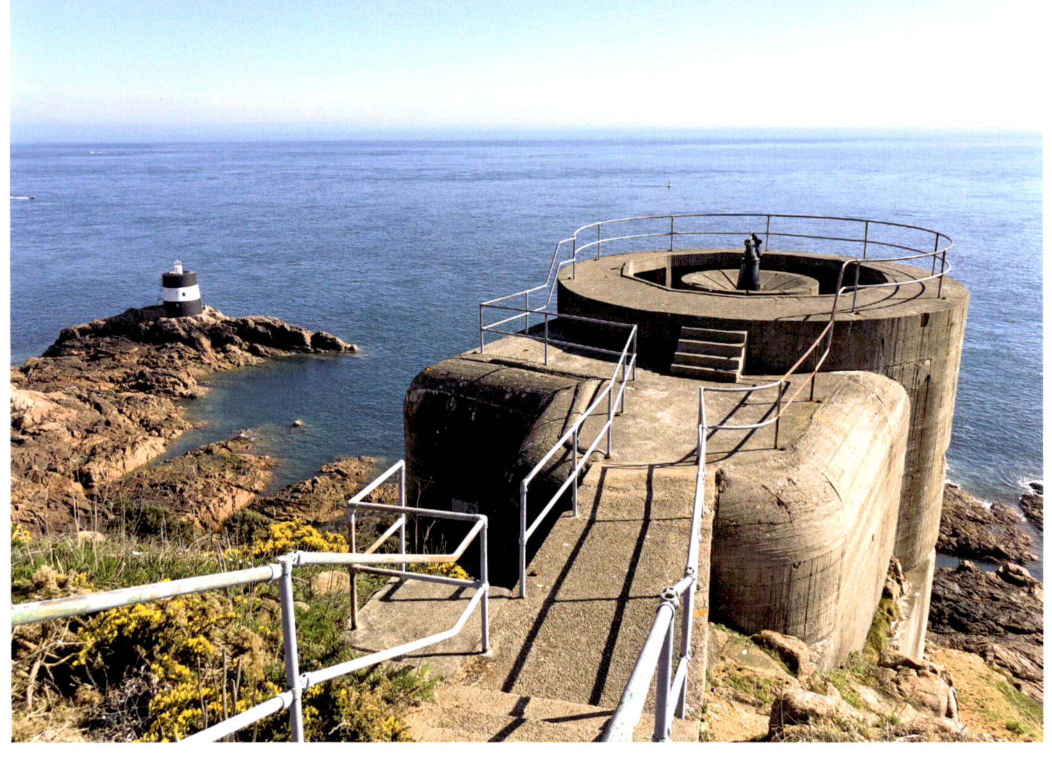

MP1 Naval Direction and Range-Finding Tower. (Author's collection)

Batterie Moltke

Batterie Moltke was another of Hitler's coastal batteries constructed on Jersey during the Second World War. Foreign workers from the Organisation Todt (OT) were brought across from mainland Europe to the north-west corner of the island at the Les Landes headland, where they stayed in a workers' camp around 1 mile to the east of the site that we can still see today. The first big guns arrived in March 1941 in the form of two captured medium French field guns that were essentially of First World War standard. The original plan was for the navy to man the coastal artillery batteries, but it was actually the army who took possession of the site in May 1941, with two further 15.5 cm guns being transferred here in July 1941. With a range of approximately 10 miles, these four guns were placed in open circular positions but just a year later in the summer of 1942, a series of modernisations took place to allow the battery to have more modern 15 cm turreted naval guns. These Nos 1 to 4 Gun positions were identical in their design and layout, with a staggering 80 cm thick reinforced concrete floor, and were constructed over the next ten months with the last being completed in April 1943. Each position had three ammunition elevators, three gun crew access points, three storage areas, drainage pumps and a seemingly endless length of passageways.

Although these gun positions are the main focal point of the battery, and understandably so, there were numerous of other associated buildings constructed. Large personnel bunkers, each accommodating up to twenty-seven men, were 'attached' to each gun position and they had a central heating boiler as well as a mechanical ventilation. Reserve ammunition bunkers were dotted across the site and, incredibly, these were all connected to the gun emplacements via a huge network of interconnecting underground tunnels. Around ten barrack huts were built, along with three anti-aircraft positions, complete with their own ammunition store and crew shelter. One anti-tank and three heavy machine gun emplacements were constructed, along with six machine gun nests and a staggering fourteen fixed flamethrower positions. On the cliff edge, a powerful coastal artillery searchlight and the Coastal Artillery Range-Finding Position M2a were located, making Moltke a truly massive site. Further along the coast lies a Naval Direction and Range-Finding Tower (MP3) that was built in 1943. Its aim was to control and direct the fire from the coastal batteries by working in unison with the other eight Range-Finding Towers that had been planned for Jersey – although only three were actually completed.

The 5th Battery Army Coastal Artillery Regiment 1265 were responsible for the daily operations at Moltke, with around a hundred men stationed here at its peak. Despite the vast number of resources put into the site, Moltke saw very limited action outside of its live firing exercises. The Allies knew full well the capabilities of the battery and simply avoided getting into close proximity with it. In one way, it meant that sea around this part of Jersey was indeed under German control, but certainly as the war went on, the large number of troops here were simply being bypassed and became largely a redundant part of the war

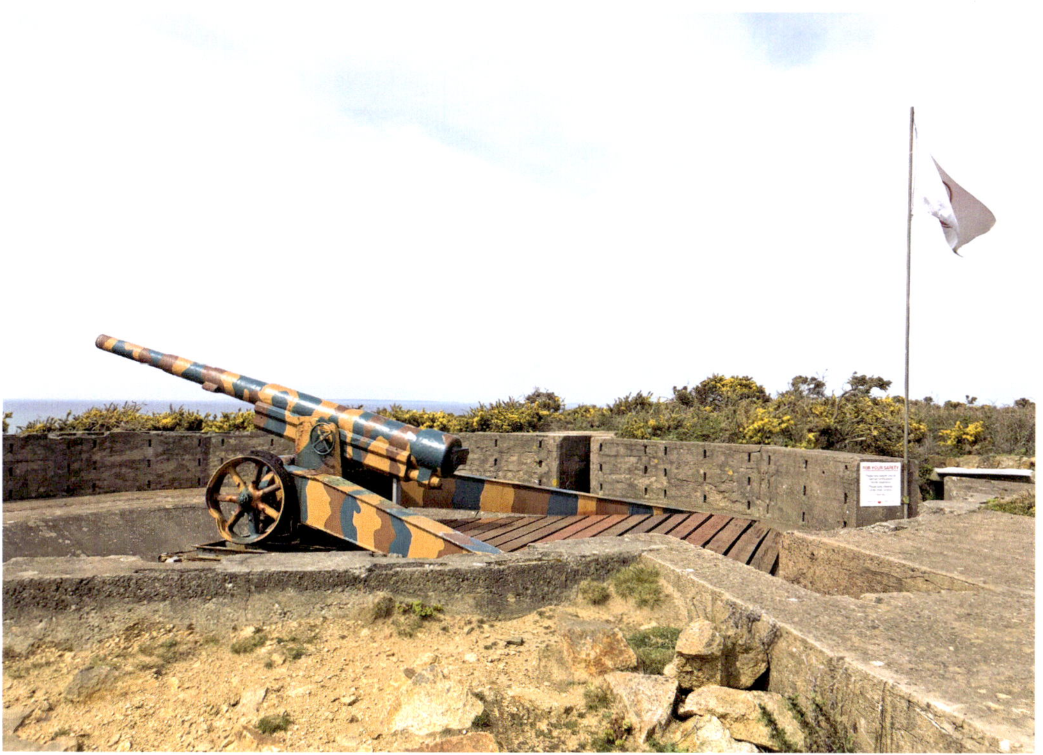

The army artillery emplacement at No. 4 Gun position at Batterie Moltke. (Author's collection)

effort. In the days and months after D-Day, the battery did engage with Allied shipping, laying down heavy fire on a number of occasions.

When Jersey was liberated on 9 May 1945, the men stationed here were taken as prisoners of war, and the liberating forces removed the large guns and simply threw them over the cliffs. Anything that could be reused from the myriad of bunkers and emplacements was taken, and the site was left open for mother nature to reclaim. In the years that followed, the area became a dumping ground for all sorts of things and, ultimately, the gun emplacements were filled in and buried. In 1978, the Channel Islands Occupation Society (CIOS) were made custodians of No. 4 Gun position and have done a sterling job in the years that have followed in excavating and preserving this part of the site. The footprint of Batterie Moltke covers a great swathe of land and is freely accessible to everyone throughout the year. It is possible to explore several concrete structures that are above ground, whilst the other three main gun emplacements remain completely buried, apart from their concrete gun platforms which lie on the surface. However, No. 4 Gun position has been cleaned out and is regularly opened by CIOS members, offering a tantalising glimpse into the engineering that built this site and what daily life would have been like here for German forces during the Second World War.

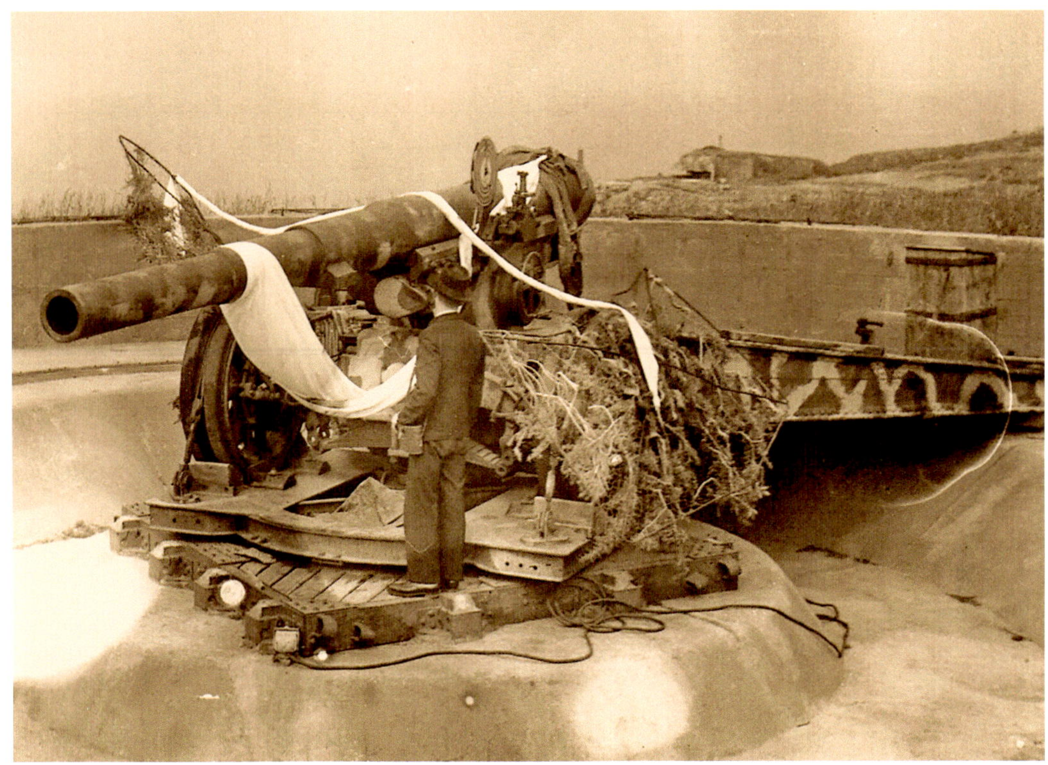

No. 4 Gun in May 1945 after liberation – the white sheet was placed across the barrel by the German forces stationed there to show they were surrendering. (Courtesy of the Channel Island Occupation Society (Jersey))

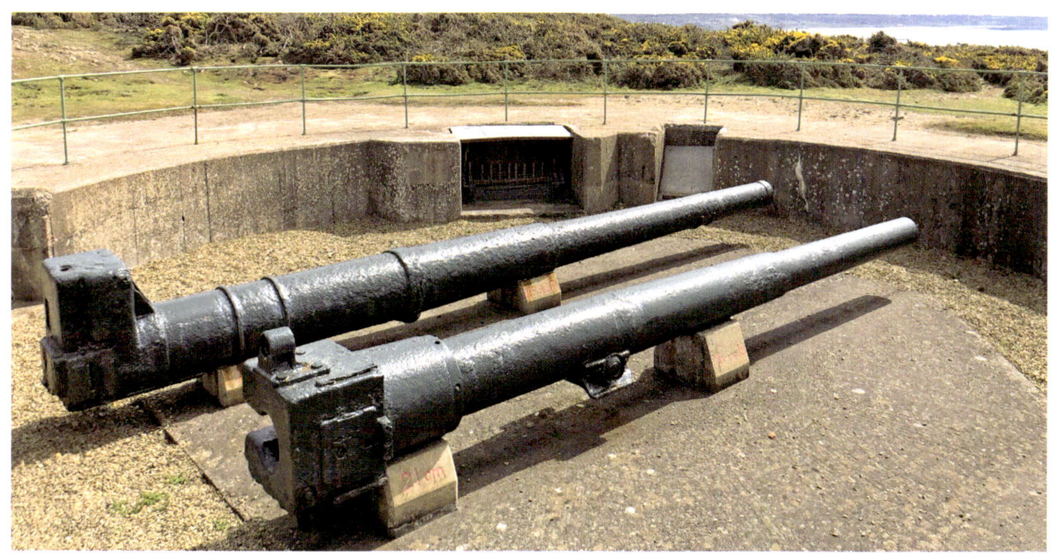

Two barrels lay in the naval gun emplacement at No. 4 Gun. (Author's collection)

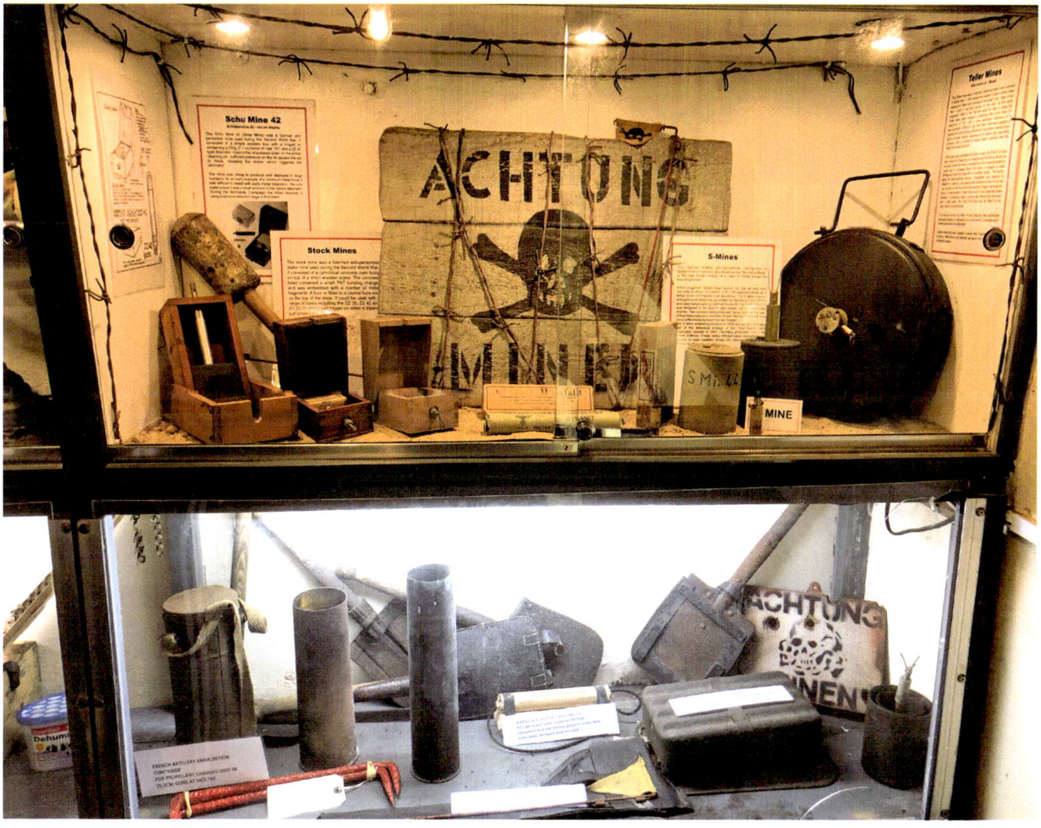

The internal rooms of the gun position are full of artefacts from the occupation. (Author's collection)

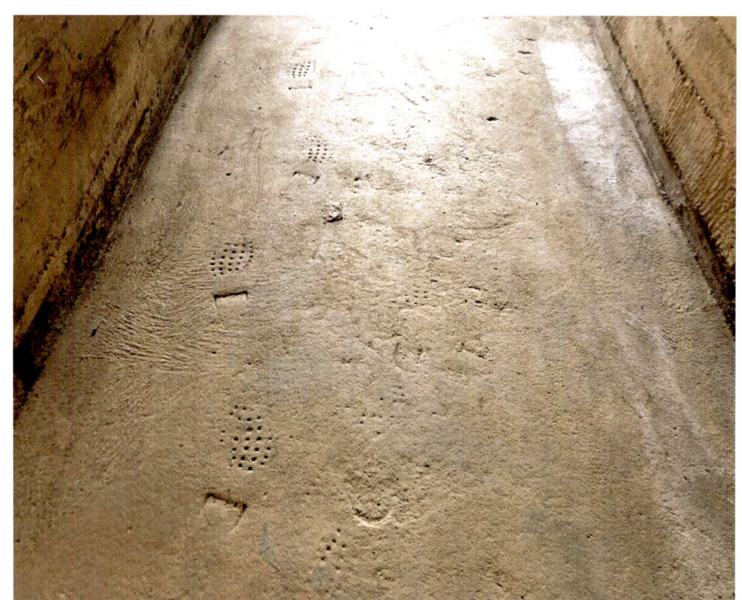

As you exit No. 4 Gun position you can make out the boot imprints of the workers who laid the original concrete. (Author's collection)

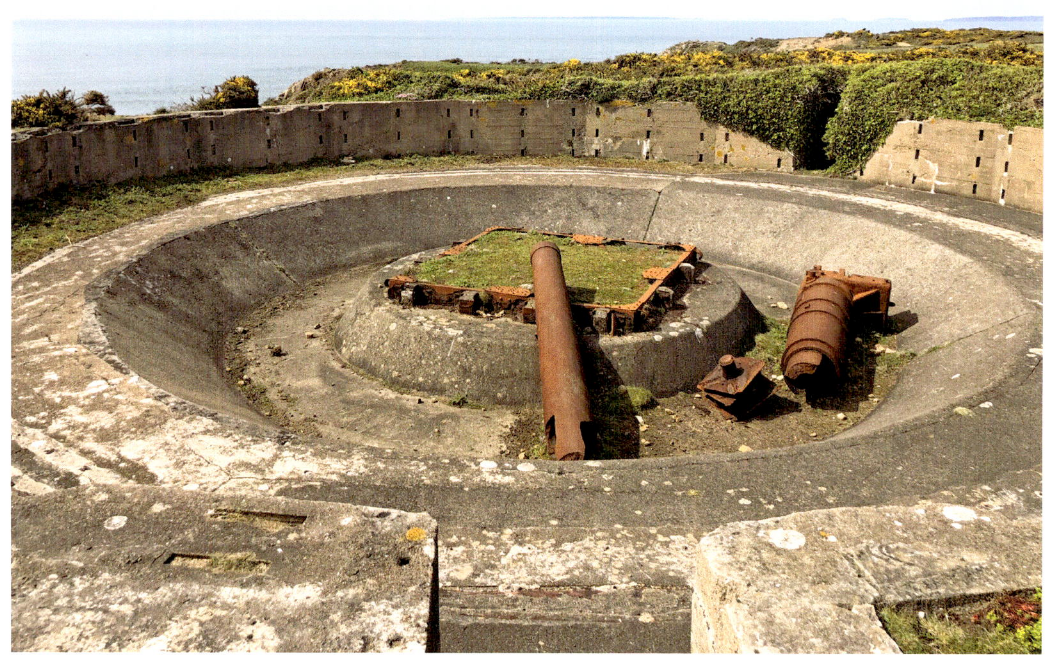

Although the remainder of the vast site has been left to nature, it is still possible to find further relics across the Les Landes site. (Author's collection)

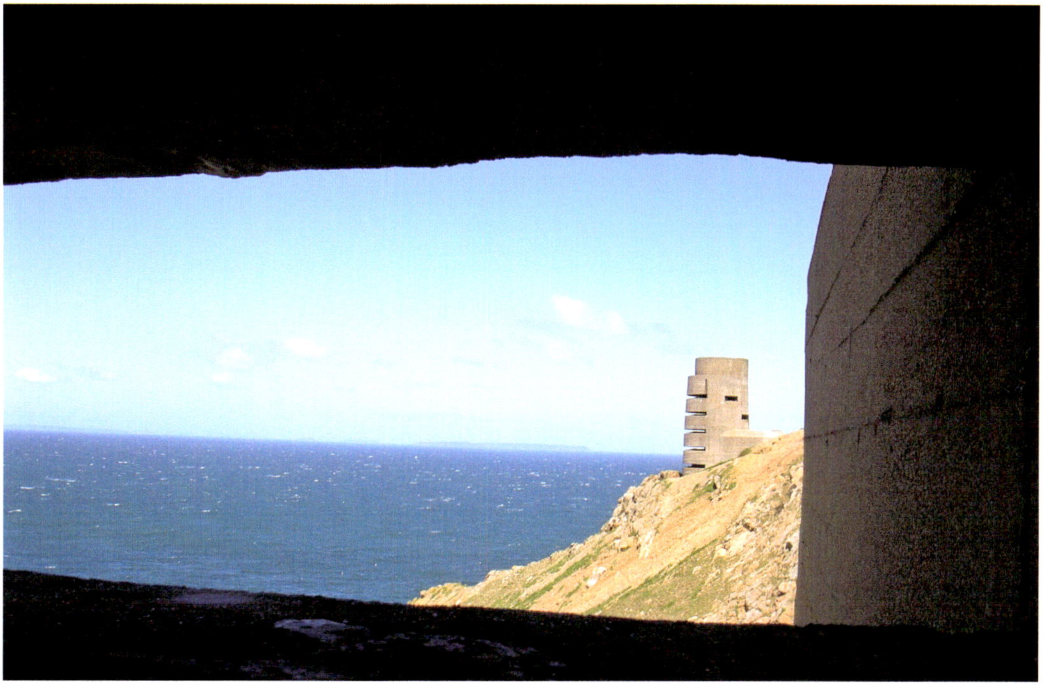

A view of MP3 from the Coastal Artillery Range-Finding Position. (Author's collection)

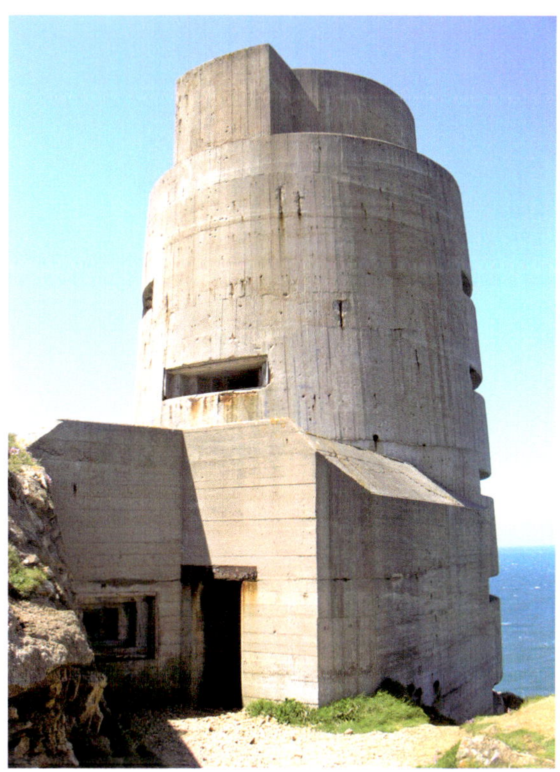

MP3 Naval Direction and
Range-Finding Tower.
(Author's collection)

Batterie Roon

Another of the coastal batteries built by German forces during the occupation, Batterie Roon was armed with four 22 cm guns and worked in coordination with the other coastal batteries from its location in the south-west of the island. The site of Batterie Roon has long since gone, being redeveloped in the years after the war with housing estates and the prison, although a small part of it is recognisable within a communal park area.

Battle of Jersey

Between 1778 and 1783 tensions between England and France were at such a low the two nations were fighting what was known as the Anglo-French War. The Channel Islands were an obvious location of strategic importance between the two countries and large numbers of privateers operated from here, regularly causing havoc amongst French merchant shipping. The war provided the French government with an opportunity to put a stop to this.

In July 1778, King George III granted the necessary funds to build a series of thirty new defensive round towers across the island to help bolster the existing forts and gun batteries, as well as sending additional troops to the islands to assist the Jersey Militia with the defence of the island. However, the vast majority of these proposed new towers were not built in time, as on 1 May 1779, a French force attempted a landing at St Ouen's Bay. This was spotted by lookouts who were able to notify the 78th Seaforth Highlanders and Jersey Militia, who in turn were able to prevent a landing.

Despite this setback, the French were determined to attack again, and around 2,000 soldiers left Granville on 5 January 1781 to attack the island. Although some troops were lost during the crossing, well over 1,250 of these soldiers made it across and landed undetected at La Rocque, Grouville, that evening and the following morning. At least 700 men marched the few kilometres to St Helier, arriving in the morning and setting up defensive positions in the market while most of the town was asleep. In fact, they surrounded Government House and surprised the island's governor, Major Moses Corbet, who was still in bed! Now captured, the French asked Corbet to order the commander at Elizabeth Castle to surrender, which he signed in an effort to avoid any further harm to St Helier.

However, those at Elizabeth Castle had other ideas, with Captain Mulcaster C.R.E., the commander at Elizabeth Castle, refusing the request to surrender and opening fire on the French. Command of the island had now passed to the next most senior British commander, twenty-four-year-old Major Francis Peirson, who was in charge of the troops at Saint Peter's Barracks. He assembled his men and Jersey militia to the west of the town, sending the 78th Seaforth Highlanders to the Mont de la Ville hill (the current location of Fort Regent) to block any possible French retreat, before taking his remaining troops to attack. As they reached the edge of the town, the French sent Corbet to tell them that if they did not capitulate the French troops would ransack the town within half an hour. Peirson's reply was to tell them they had twenty minutes to surrender. The British troops marched into the town and easily outnumbered the French troops there. The fighting was short and many of the French surrendered when their commander was wounded.

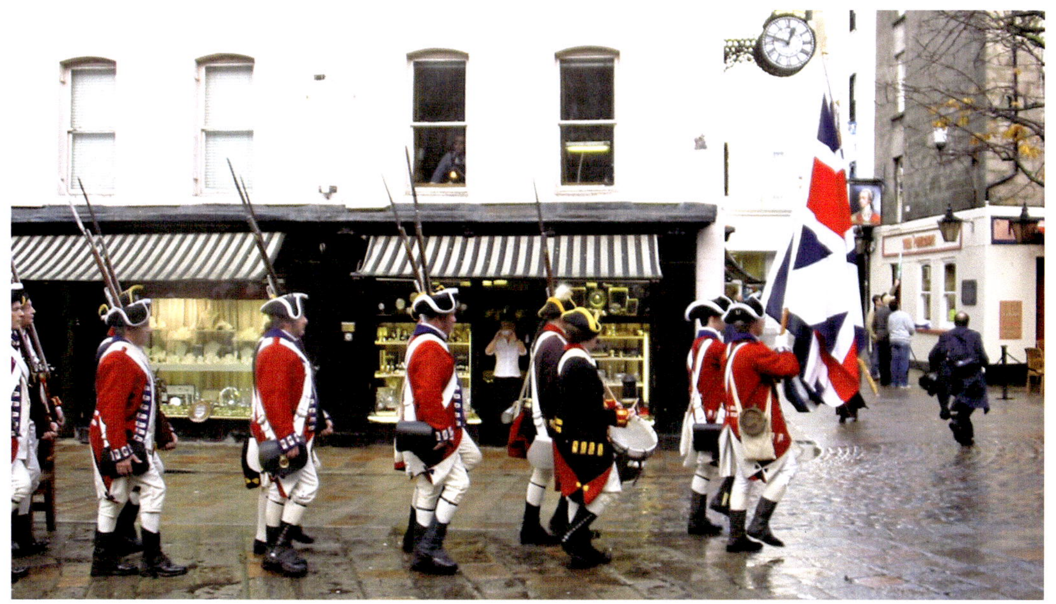

A re-enactment of the 1781 Jersey Militia marching in the Royal Square, St Helier, the site of the Battle of Jersey, during ceremonies marking the anniversary of the battle on 6 January 2007. To the right of the photograph is the house where French commander Baron de Rullecourt died, now a pub called *The Peirson*. (Public domain)

By the end of the day, the French expedition force lost almost half of its fighting force and was defeated. It is estimated that around 150 were killed or wounded, with 600 being taken prisoner, whilst the British had approximately seventy injured or killed. Both the French commander, Baron Philippe de Rullecourt, and the British commander, Major Peirson, were killed. He was buried in the parish church of St Helier, and a marble monument was erected in his memory. Following this action, the government built nineteen more of Conway's recommended round towers and three Martello towers over the next thirty years to improve the island's defences.

Channel Islands Military Museum

Located towards the northern end of St Ouen's Bay, the Channel Islands Military Museum is actually housed in a former 10.5 cm casemate that was part of Hitler's Atlantic Wall defences on the island. Nestled alongside the seawall, the 10.5 cm gun overlooked the wide expanse of sand that stretched for 3 miles along Jersey's west coast. During the Nazi occupation of 1940–45, a twelve-man crew would have manned the position day and night, and the fact that the museum building itself is one of the exhibits only adds to the impressive nature of the collection. Inside, every inch is used to showcase German and civilian items from the occupation. From uniforms to guns, ordinance to official documentation, and plenty of personal items and recounts, this is a museum that tells the story of what life was like for the local population under five years of occupation.

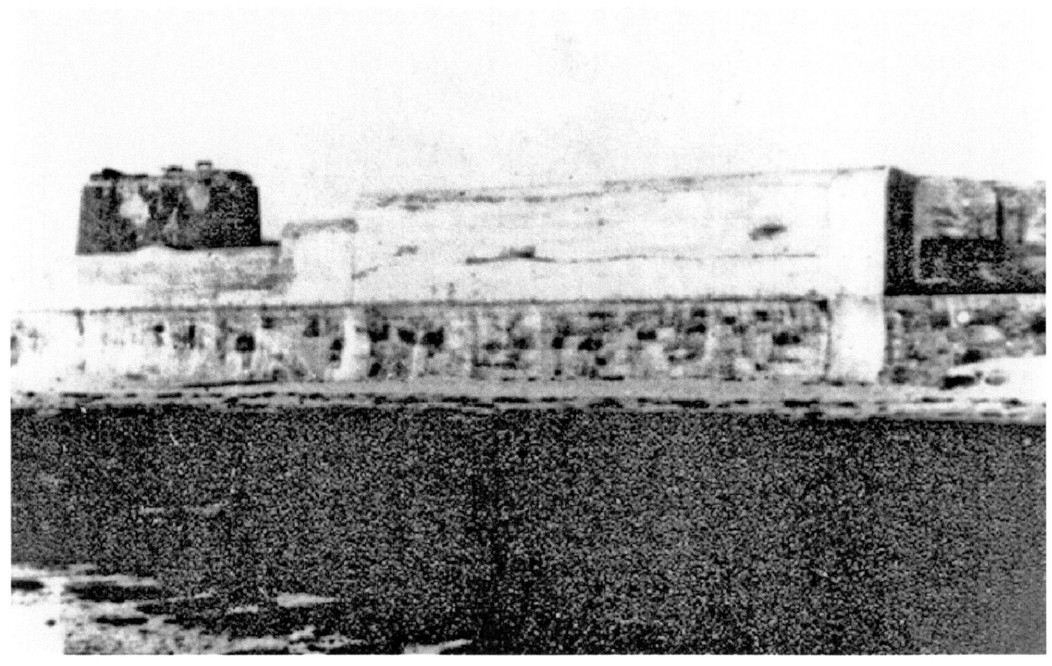

One of only two known photographs of the 10.5 cm casemate during the occupation. (Courtesy of Damien Horn, The Channel Islands Military Museum)

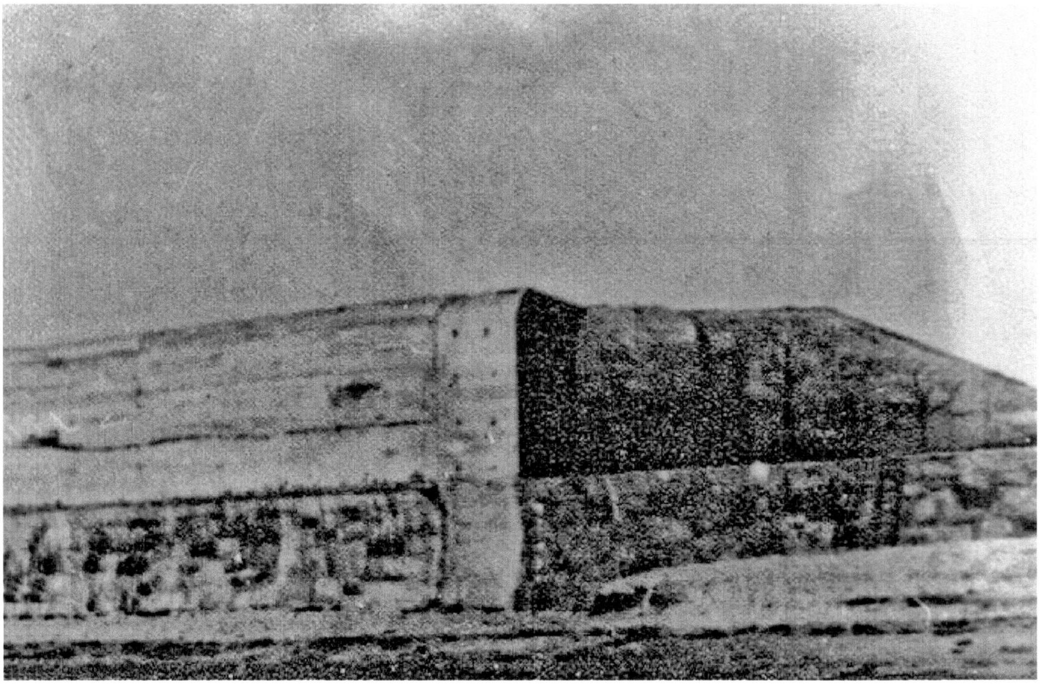

In this second wartime picture, it is just possible to make out camouflaged trees painted on the defensive wall! (Courtesy of Damien Horn, The Channel Islands Military Museum)

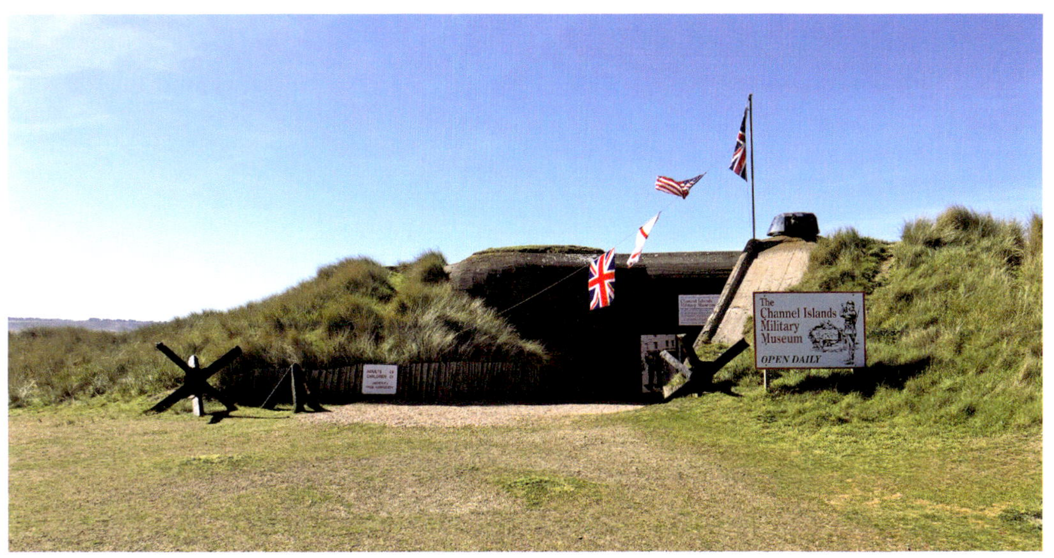

A view of the bunker today – now The Channel Islands Military Museum. (Author's collection)

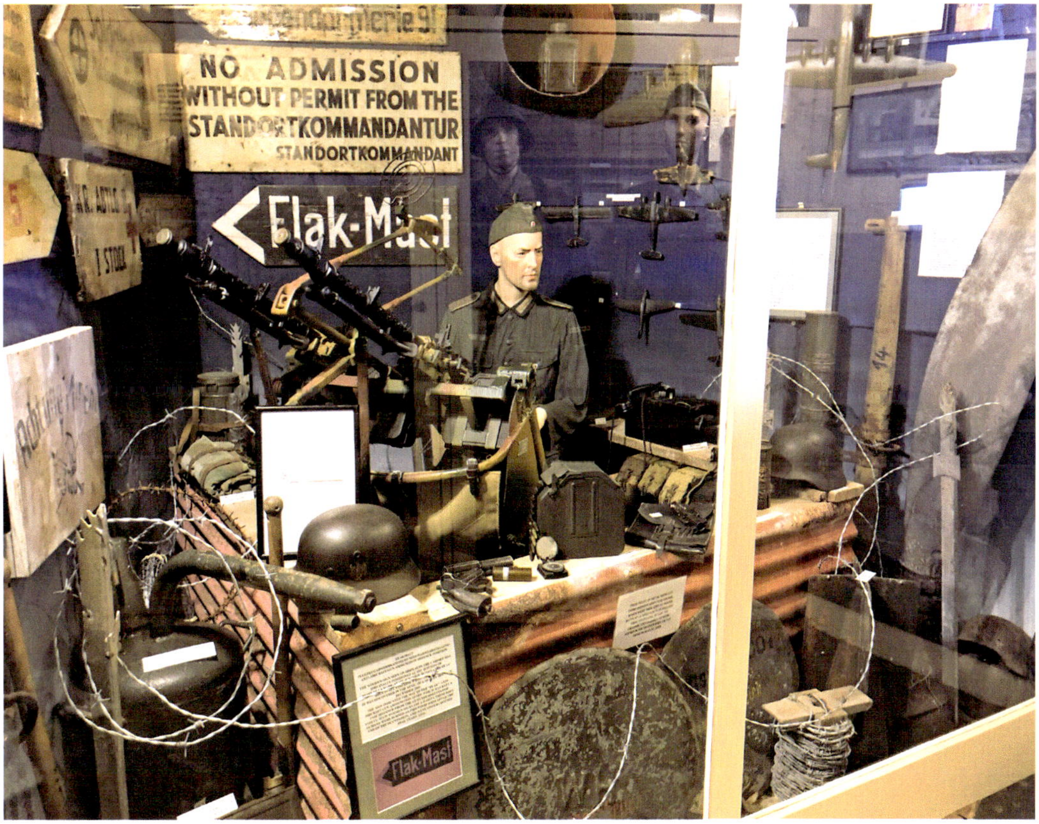

Each room inside the bunker is jam-packed with artefacts from the occupation. (Author's collection)

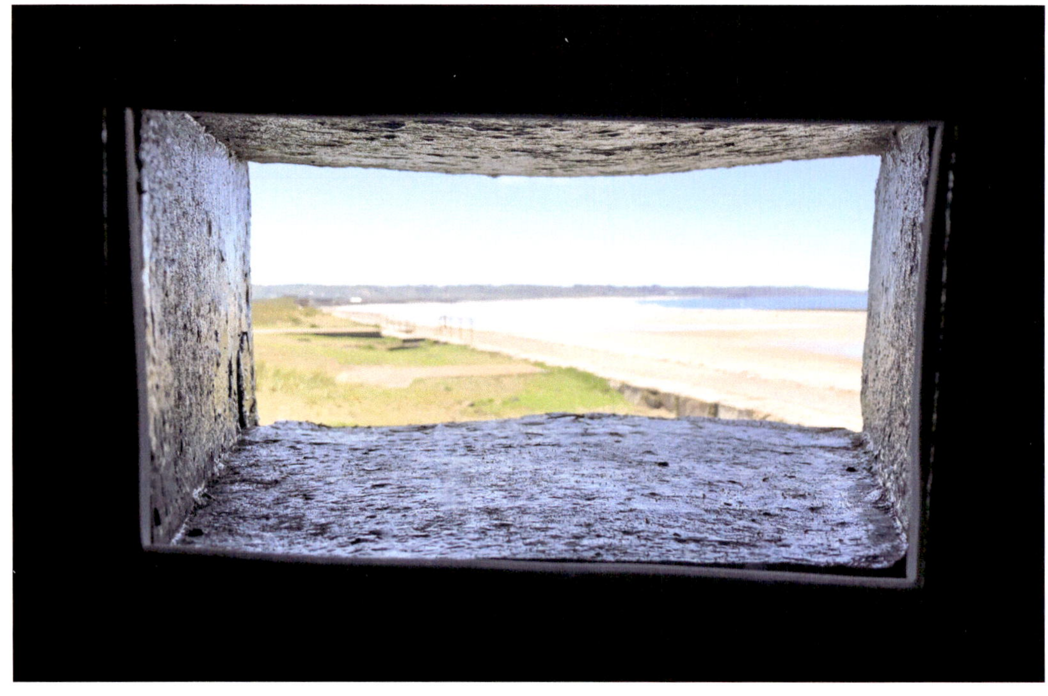

A view across St Ouen's Bay from inside the casemate. (Author's collection)

Elizabeth Castle

There can be few military locations as spectacular as Elizabeth Castle!

Lying within St Aubin's Bay and a stone's throw away from the capital St Helier is a small island that is cut off from the mainland by the tide twice a day called L'Islet. Adjacent to this, is a small outcrop of rocks where a Belgium monk named Helerius landed in around AD 550 and established a small hermitage. From here, he converted Jersey's population to Christianity, before later being killed by sea-going raiders, and from this point the hermitage became a prominent place of pilgrimage. Centuries later, in 1155, an Abbey of Saint Helier was founded on L'Islet, and remained operating until it was forcibly closed at the Reformation. The Crown seized the monastic buildings, and they were then fortified to create a new defensive position.

The development of weaponry in the sixteenth century meant that the existing stronghold on the island at Mont Orgueil was no longer sufficient to defend Jersey. A newer, stronger bastion was needed, and with the vital port of St Helier now vulnerable from attack by ships armed with new cannons, the tidal island of L'Islet, sat at the mouth of the harbour, seemed the perfect place to build.

Work developing the site began in 1594, with the Upper Ward and the Queen Elizabeth Gate being completed first. Once complete, Sir Walter Raleigh, who was the Governor of Jersey between 1600 and 1603, named the castle *Elizabeth Castle* after Queen Elizabeth I of England, and moved the Governor's official place of residence from Mont Orgueil to the new castle. The building work was far from over however, and by 1636 the Lower Ward was constructed on what was the site of the former abbey church – with a portion of the former church now becoming a storeroom. A large barrack building, along with a separate officers' quarters, were built around a central parade ground, and wells and cisterns were dug into the rock for water.

When the English Civil War erupted in 1642, it wasn't long before the great stronghold of Elizabeth Castle became embroiled with it. In March 1643, Sir Philippe de Carteret, the Seigneur of St Ouen and also the island's Lieutenant Governor and Bailiff, retreated to the castle after a number of locals prevented him from reading out a letter from the king to the States and in the April of that year, the castle's guns opened fire on nearby Parliamentarian ships in the bay. Sir Philippe died in August 1643, and his son-in-law Sir George Carteret took over his roles. He managed to reduce and expel the Parliamentarian faction.

Between April and June 1646, Charles, the Prince of Wales, visited the castle and then returned three years later in September 1649 as King Charles II. He was the eldest surviving child of Charles I, who had been executed in January 1649. The Parliament of Scotland proclaimed Charles II king on 5 February 1649, and a few days later, on 17 February 1649, the Bailiff of Jersey, George Carteret, also proclaimed him king, as well as offering him asylum on the island. Knowing that Carteret had a small private army made up of Royalist veterans who had fled from England after the defeat of Charles I, along with a collection of foreign mercenaries, he accepted, and moved into Elizabeth Castle.

In October 1651, Parliamentarian forces inevitably landed in Jersey and bombarded the castle with mortars. Admiral Blake's fleet escorted over 2,500 troops to the island and lay siege to the area. Besieged for seven weeks, a shell crashed through the roof of the old medieval abbey church in the heart of the castle complex, which had been used as the storehouse for ammunition and provisions, and two years of supplies were gone. Carteret was forced to surrender on 15 December 1651 and Jersey was then held by the Parliamentarians for the next nine years until the restoration of the monarchy.

The strategic location of the castle saw more improvements added to it, which only enhanced its reputation as Jersey's foremost defensive position. During the Seven Years' War (1756–63), French prisoners were kept at the island, and a few years later during the Battle of Jersey in 1781, the castle garrison refused to surrender to the French, who were eventually defeated. However, this incident highlighted the potential weakness of a castle that is surrounded by sea for seven hours out of every twelve, as it meant that the troops at Elizabeth Castle were unable to effectively defend St Helier when cut-off by the tide. This vulnerability led to the construction of Fort Regent on Mont de la Ville, and this in time became the site of the main British garrison.

In the early nineteenth century a two-storey hospital was built, as well as a breakwater linking L'Islet to Hermitage Rock. At the turn of the twentieth century, the castle's usefulness as a military location diminished significantly, and the British government withdrew the garrison and sold the castle to the States of Jersey in 1923 for £1,500, who then opened the site to the public as a museum.

It did see a return to active service during the Second World War, when the Germans occupied the Channel Islands and used forced labourers to modernise the castle with various guns, bunkers and battlements. After the Liberation, the castle was repaired and eventually reopened to the public, run by Jersey Heritage.

Visiting Elizabeth Castle is an exhilarating experience, not just because of its size, but also because of the approach. At low tide, you can walk the causeway out to the Main Gate, whilst at all other times you will need to take an amphibious vehicle!

The castle is split into three sections: the Upper Ward, the Lower Ward and the Outer Ward. Entering through the Main Gate, there is a guard house constructed in 1810, as well as the small and much older Fort Charles, which was built in 1647 during the English Civil War. Named after the Prince of Wales, who was on the island at the time, it was constructed to cover the approach to the castle from the causeway. Further up there is the Second Gate and West Bastion, as well as the Hospital Block, built in 1810. Just below this is a searchlight bunker, constructed by German forces during the Second World War, to house a powerful searchlight that could move along rails to the North-East Bastion near the entrance. The bowling green, laid in 1640, stretches up towards the impressive Grand Battery, which was armed with fifteen 24-pound cannons, and to the side of this is a more recent 10.5 cm casemate.

The Lower Ward was constructed by 1636 and utilised the original buildings from the priory church that had been there for hundreds of years. A large parade ground dominates this section of the castle, with a large soldiers' barracks capable of accommodating a staggering 480 men in 1798 on one side, and an officers' quarters for twelve on the other. There are plenty of stores and other buildings here, with a 1940 German 10.5 cm casemate built into the Royal Bastion, which has an impressive range card painted on its walls. From the Lower Ward you can walk out to the small harbour that connects to the Hermitage.

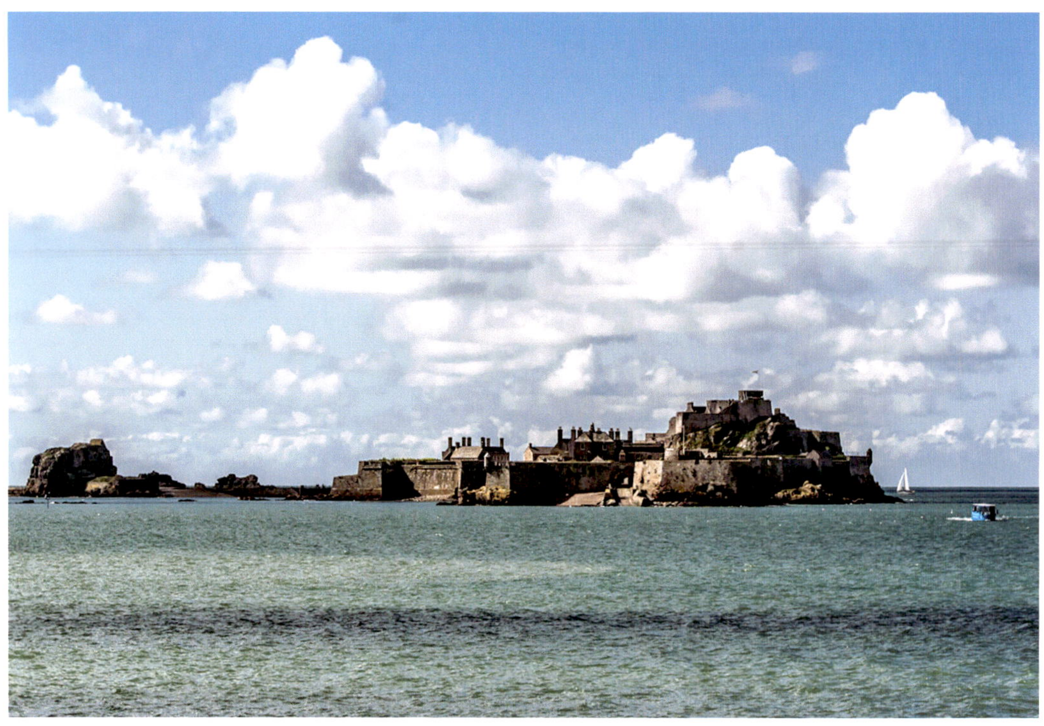

Elizabeth Castle. (Courtesy of Tobias Scheck CC BY 2.0)

The Upper Ward was the most heavily defended part of the castle and is a maze of winding stairways and narrow alleys. Passing through the Iron Gate and Queen Elizabeth Gate, complete with her coat of arms, you arrive at the lower keep, which has been embellished by a German gun position. Further around is the Captain's House and Governor's House, before you twist your way up to the Upper Keep Bastion with its two traversing guns and Mount Battery which was added to during the Second World War occupation with a fire control tower.

This is a castle with layers of history.

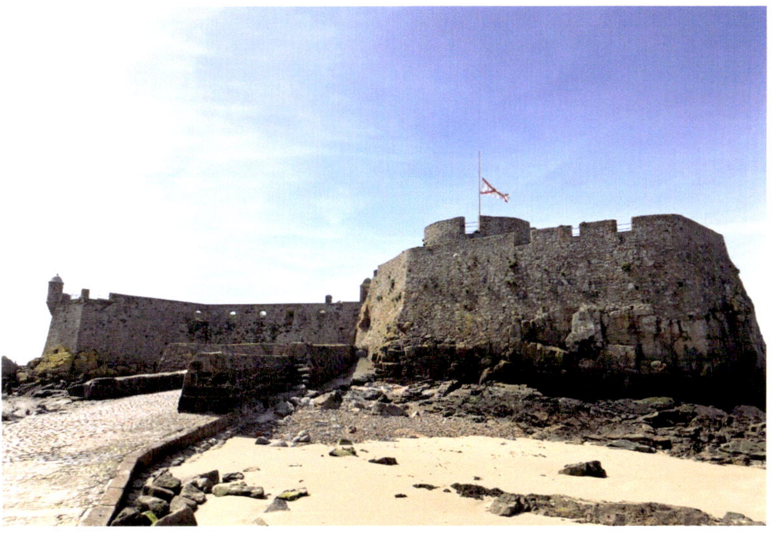

Fort Charles overlooking the causeway approach to the castle's Main Gate. (Author's collection)

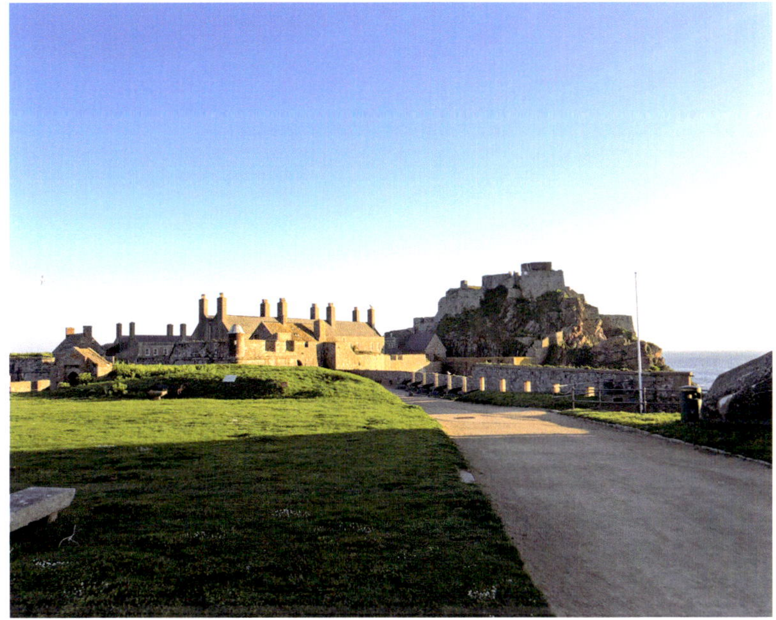

A view of the Grand Battery, with the Lower and Upper Ward behind, from the Green. (Author's collection)

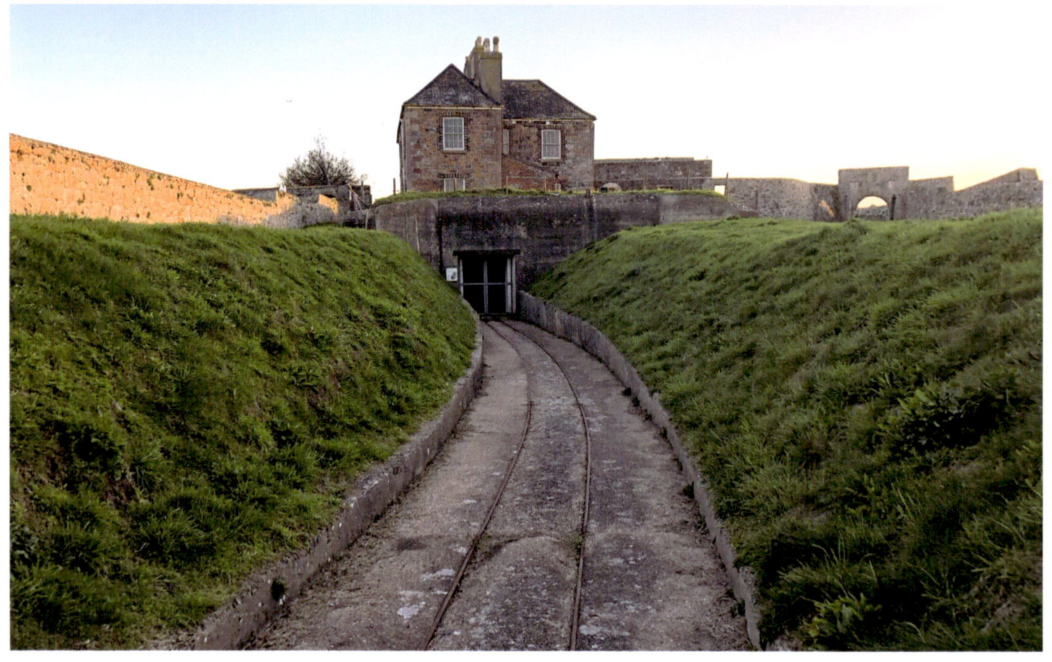

The searchlight bunker and tracks from the Second World War, with the hospital block above. (Author's collection)

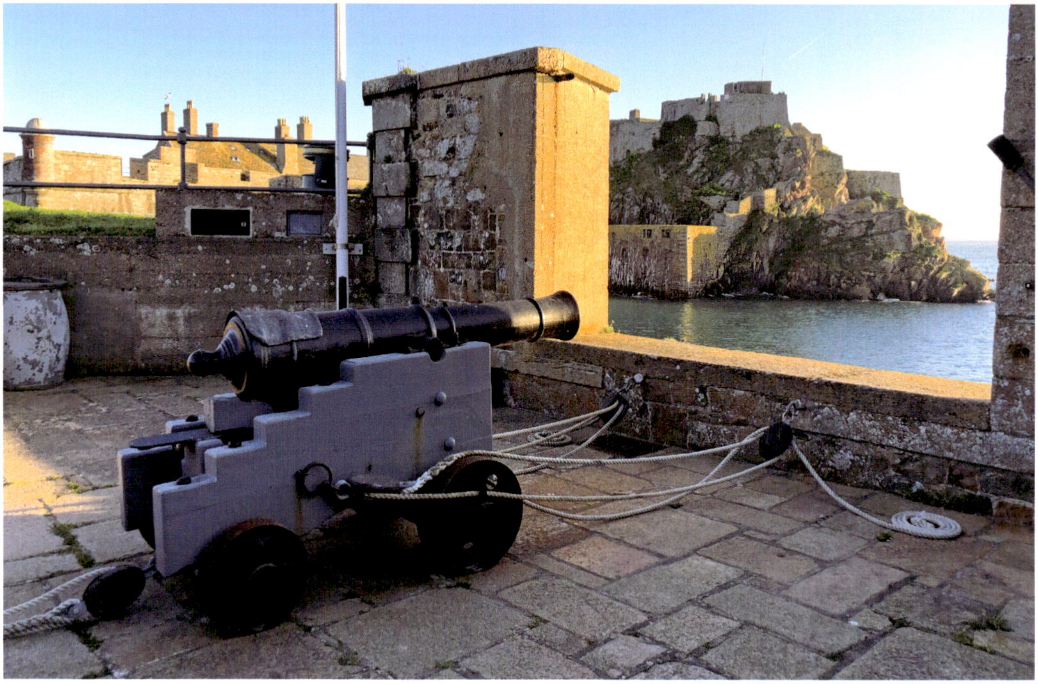

A 6-pound gun, used by re-enactors as part of their display, sits in an area known as the cockpit. (Author's collection)

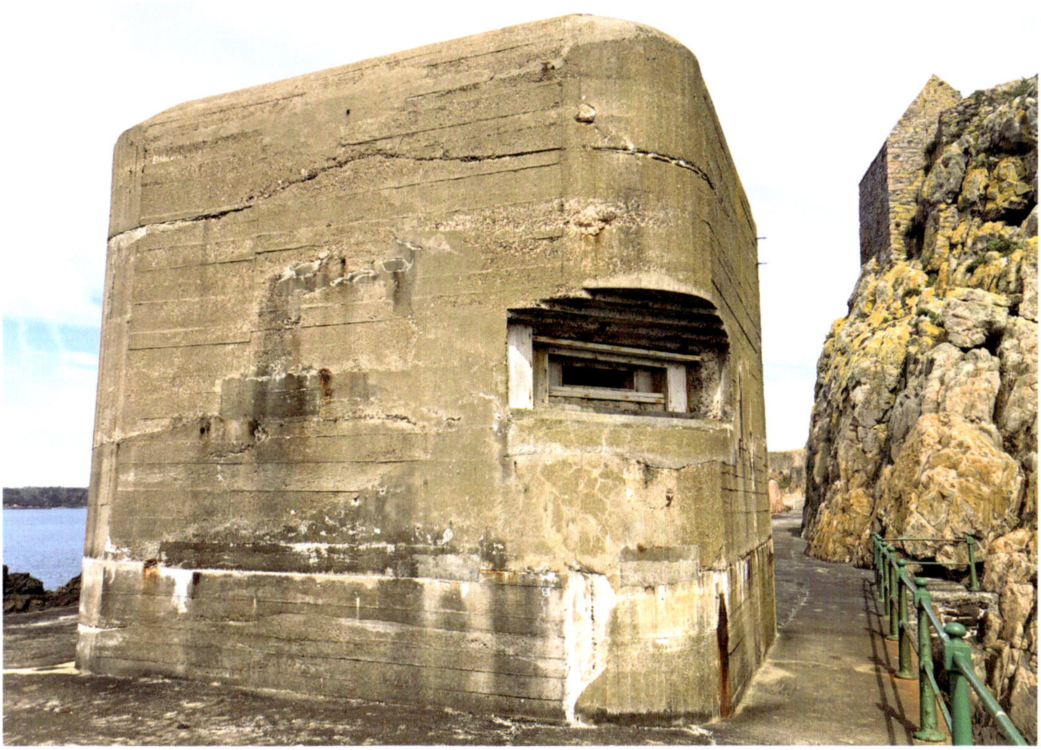

A German gun position at the end of the breakwater. (Author's collection)

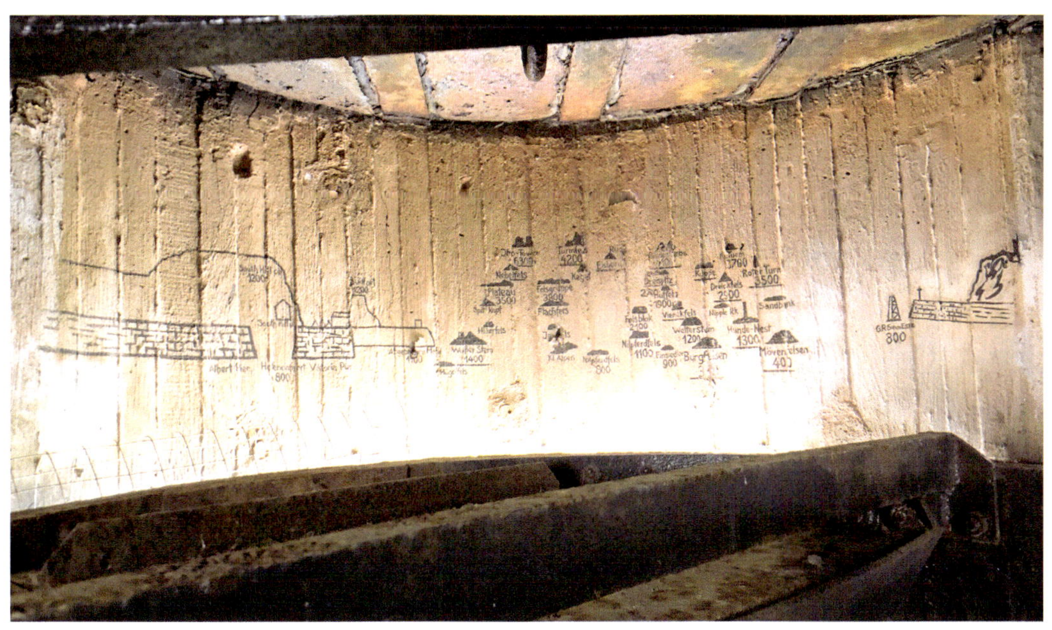

A 1940 German 10.5 cm casemate built into the Royal Bastion still has its range card painted on the walls! (Author's collection)

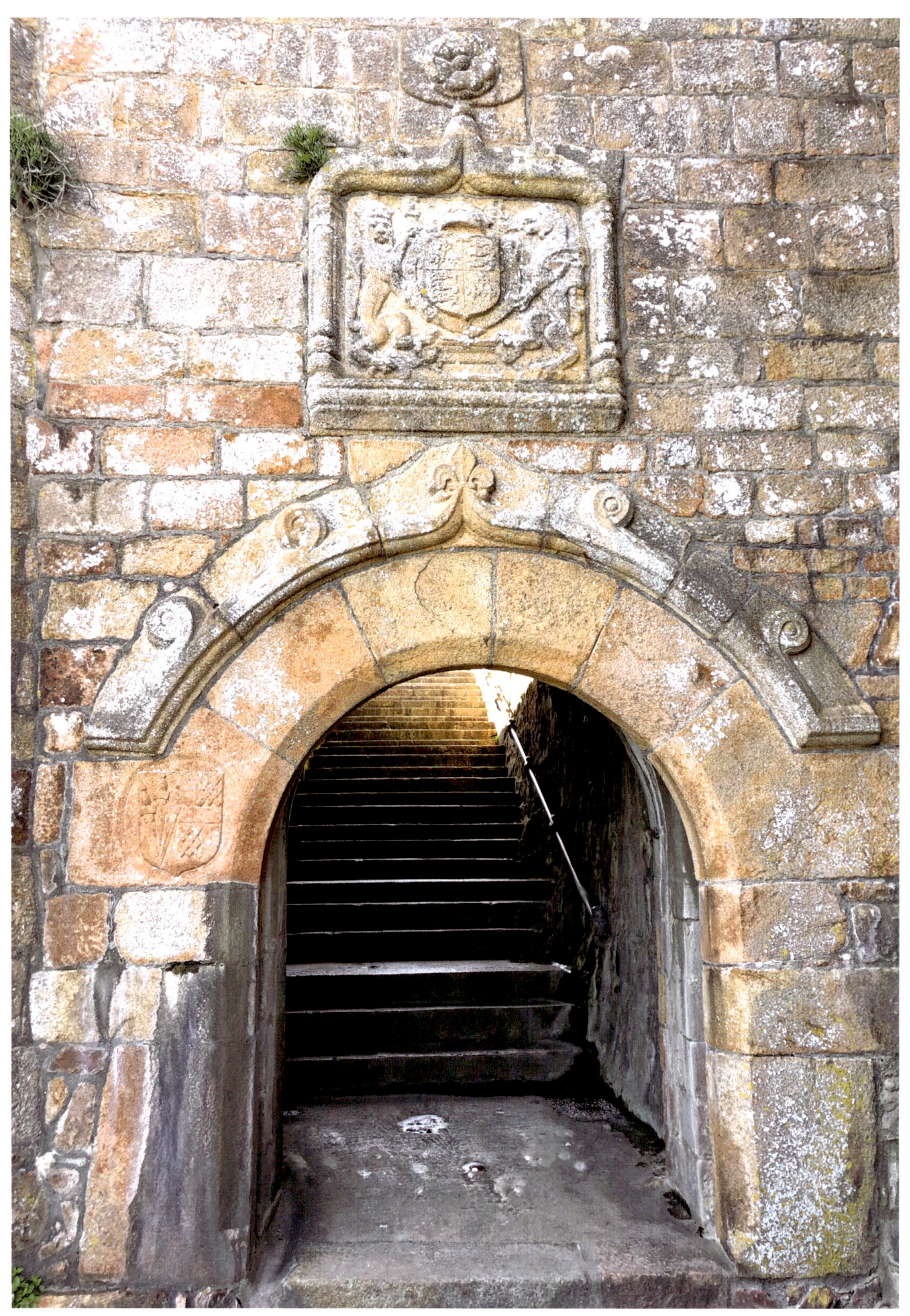

Queen Elizabeth Gate – complete with coat of arms. (Author's collection)

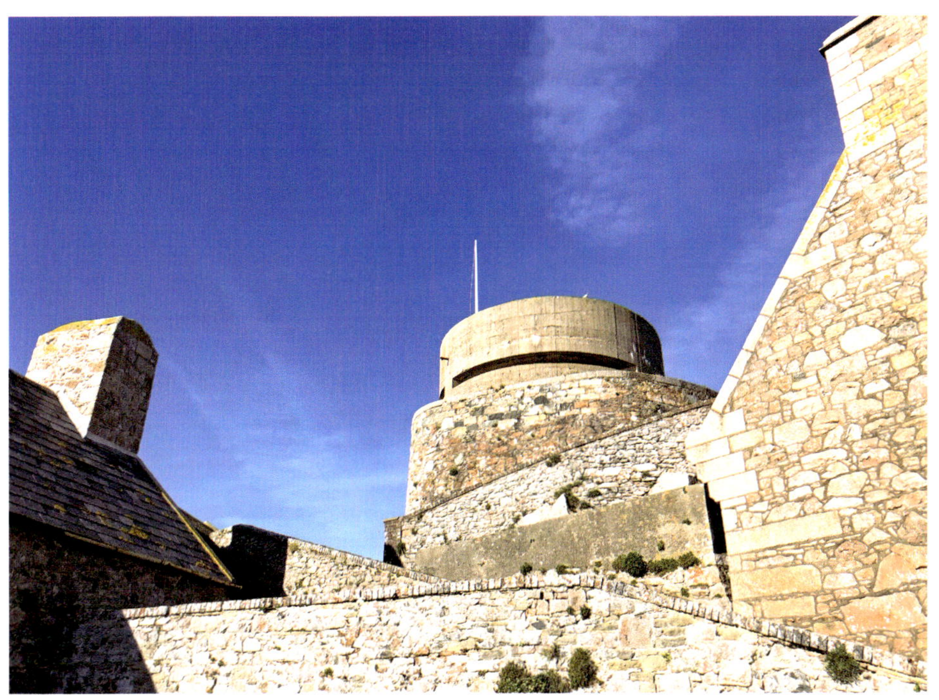

The German Fire Control Tower on the top of Mount Battery. (Author's collection)

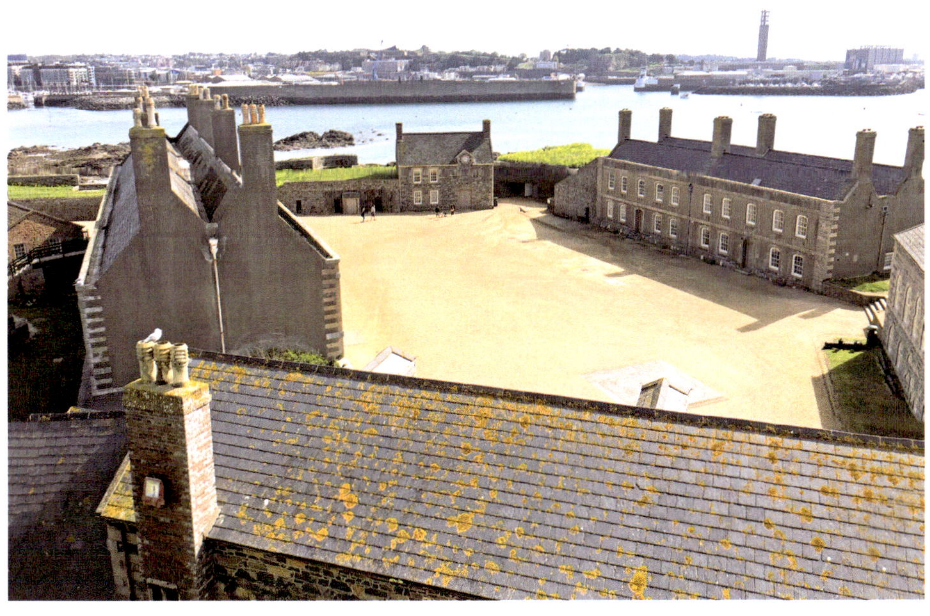

The Parade Ground, with Soldiers' Barracks on the right and Officers' Quarters on the left. (Author's collection)

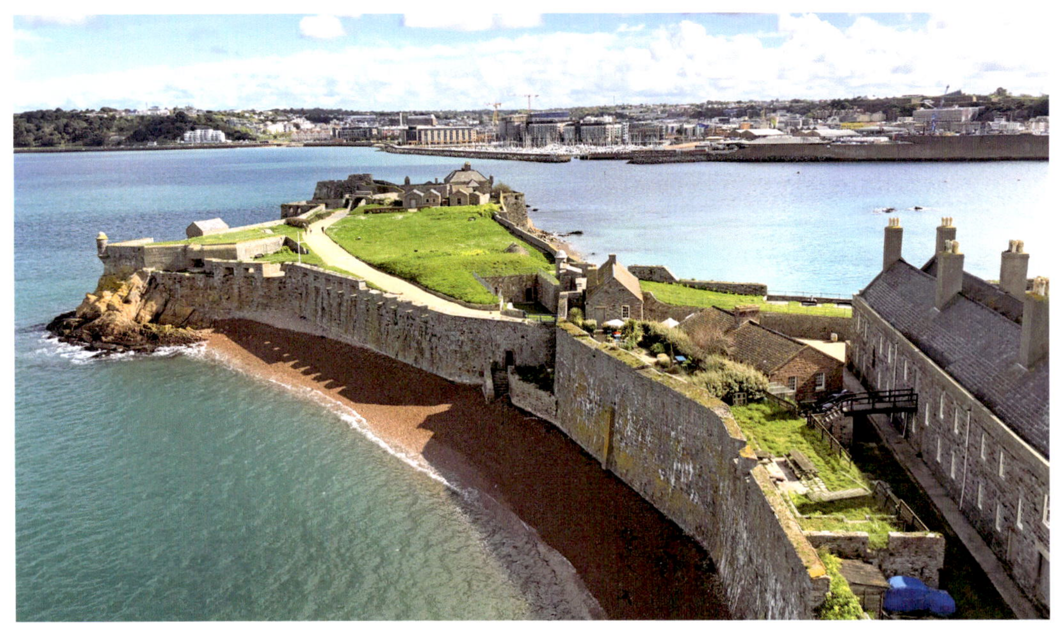

A view of the Lower Ward with St Helier in the background. (Author's collection)

Fort Henry

Built in the 1770s, Fort Henry, once known as Fort Conway, was in the sand dunes of Grouville Bay, providing a defence to this open flat stretch of land. It was the barracks of the 83rd Regiment of Foot during the Battle of Jersey in 1781 and retains the same layout today as it did then – having a large square tower as a keep, with a large yard and surrounding wall. During the Second World War, German troops modified the keep, added two platforms for searchlights, as well as constructing concrete shelters inside the yard and machine gun nests in each corner. Today, it sits within a golf course.

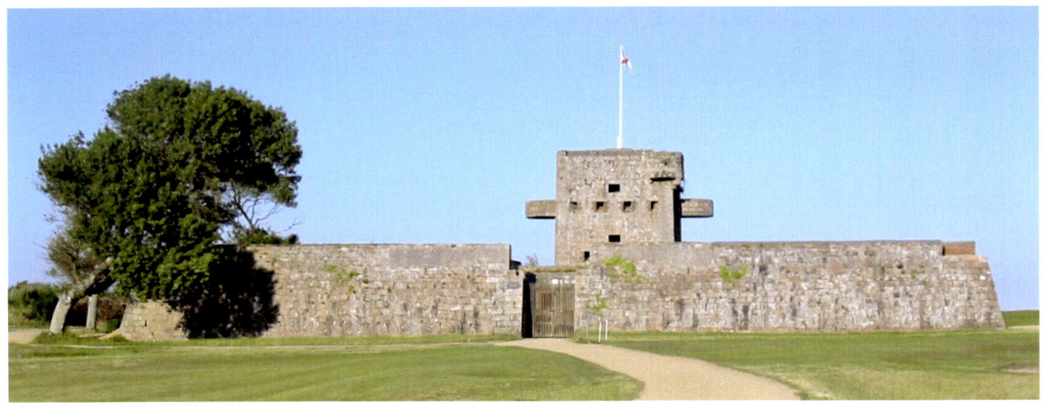

Fort Henry. (Public domain)

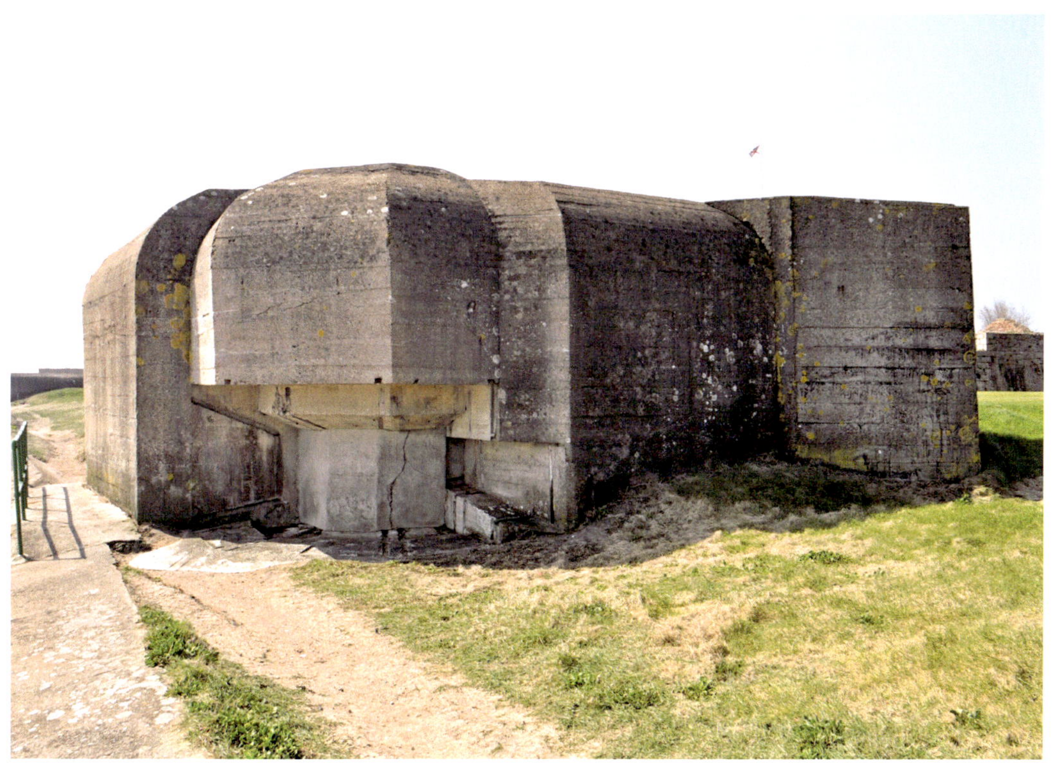

One of the German bunkers built during the Second World War. (Public domain)

Fort Leicester

Commanding the western end of Bouley Bay there has been some sort of defensive position here since 1549, when the French landed and occupied Sark, leading to the Governor of the time, Sir Anthony Paulet, advising that a gun should be placed at 'La Radde du Boullay'. Bouley Bay was of strategic importance as it was a natural haven for vessels to anchor, and by 1745, the single gun that was originally there had been added to and developed into a battery. Named after the queen's favourite, the Earl of Leicester, by 1795 it had a 12-pounder gun, along with a seaward and a landward wall and a guardhouse to the south of the site.

Fort Leicester was maintained and manned by the Jersey Militia, and by the 1830s, it was significantly improved in order to accommodate five heavy 32-pounder cannons. With a range of around 2 miles, these would have been positioned to prevent an enemy landing on the western side of Bouley Bay, and the newly constructed L'Etacquerel Fort protecting the eastern side of the bay. A company of around thirty men would have been needed to operate the weapons. During the Second World War, occupying German forces added a searchlight and more modern gun emplacements in order to protect Bouley Bay. Since then, Fort Leicester has had a number of owners, but in 2005, ownership was transferred to the Public of the Island of Jersey, and Jersey Heritage now operate the site as a heritage holiday let.

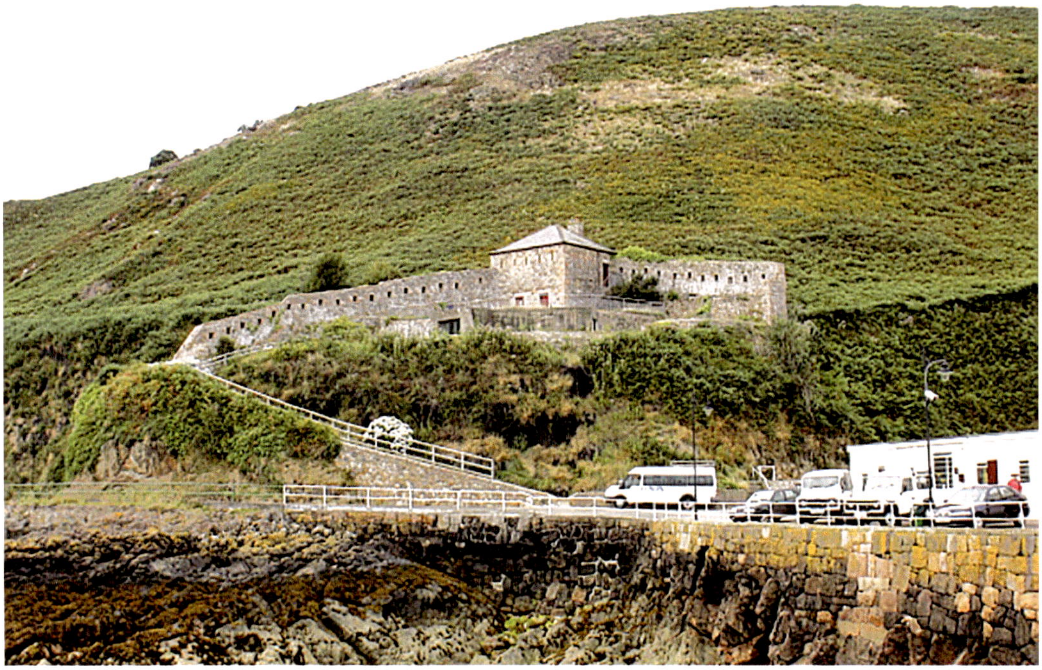

A view of Fort Leicester. (Courtesy of Bob Embleton CC BY-SA 2.0)

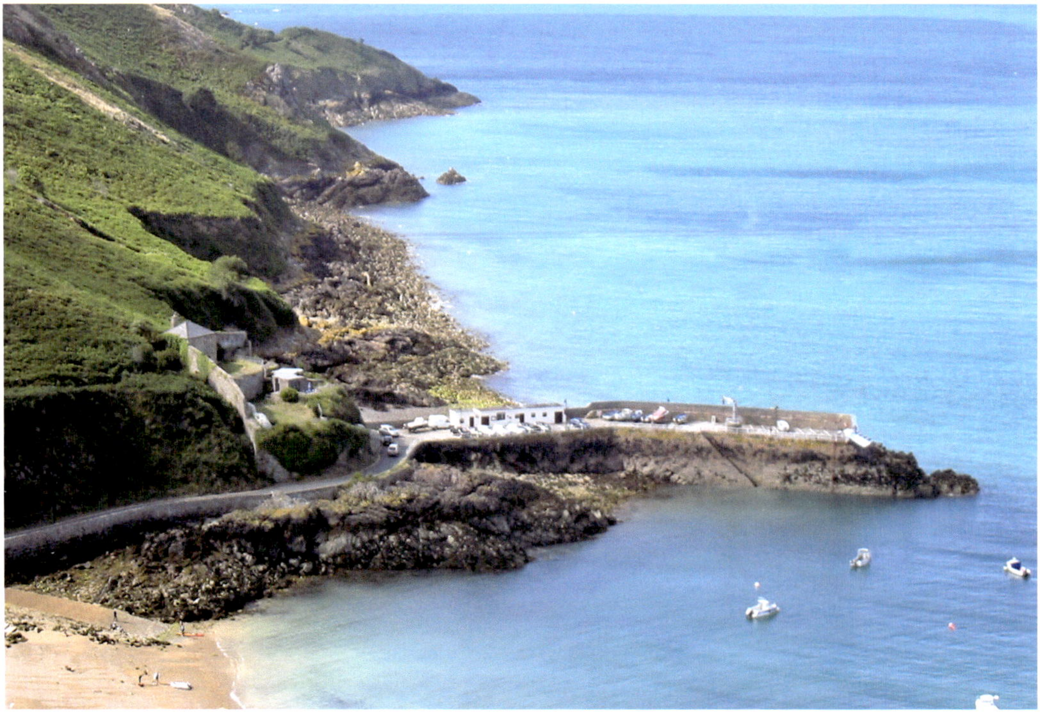

Looking down at Fort Leicester and the western side of Bouley Bay. (Public domain)

Fort Regent

In November 1806, work began on a defensive fortification in the middle of St Helier on the high ground known as Town Hill or Mont de la Ville. This high ground had previously been used by local troops in 1781 during the Battle of Jersey in order to stop the invading French force from retreating from the town, and it is a little surprising that no permanent defensive structure had not been built here before seeing as it has a commanding view over the town and harbour, although it had been used as a signal station. It was the aftermath of the Battle of Jersey and the perceived weakness of Elizabeth Castle being cut off by the tide for the majority of each day that led to a new base for the British troops being built.

Local labourers assisted the Royal Engineers over the next eight years in building a fortress that would have embrasures for over 100 cannons. Named after the Prince Regent, King George III, a 5.5-metre thick curtain wall was built on the western and eastern flanks of a large parade ground that stretched across the top. Each flank had a large bastion and there was a large ditch on the eastern side. To aid with the stability of the buildings on top, as well as the defence of the fort, a 210-metre artificial slope was constructed at the southern end, known as a glacis. As well as the bastions, Fort Regent had four redans which allowed any cannons placed there the ability to fire on any forces attacking from any direction.

Fort Regent stood watch over St Helier for the next 150 years and held the main British garrison on the island. During the Second World War, the difficult decision was made to demilitarise the islands and the Royal Militia of the Island of Jersey left the fort on 20 June 1940. It isn't surprising that the German forces who subsequently occupied the island, commandeered the fort and used it for themselves – adding flak positions to the existing structures.

After the conflict, the fort was deemed to have outlived its usefulness as a military position and was used as a storage area, and later a leisure centre, which closed in 2009.

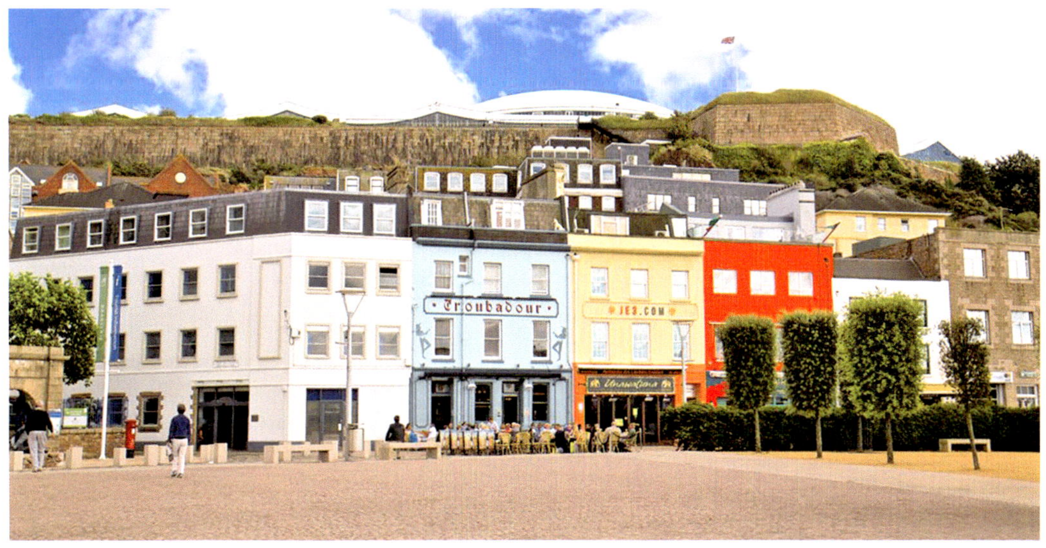

A view of the site of Fort Regent from St Helier. (Author's collection)

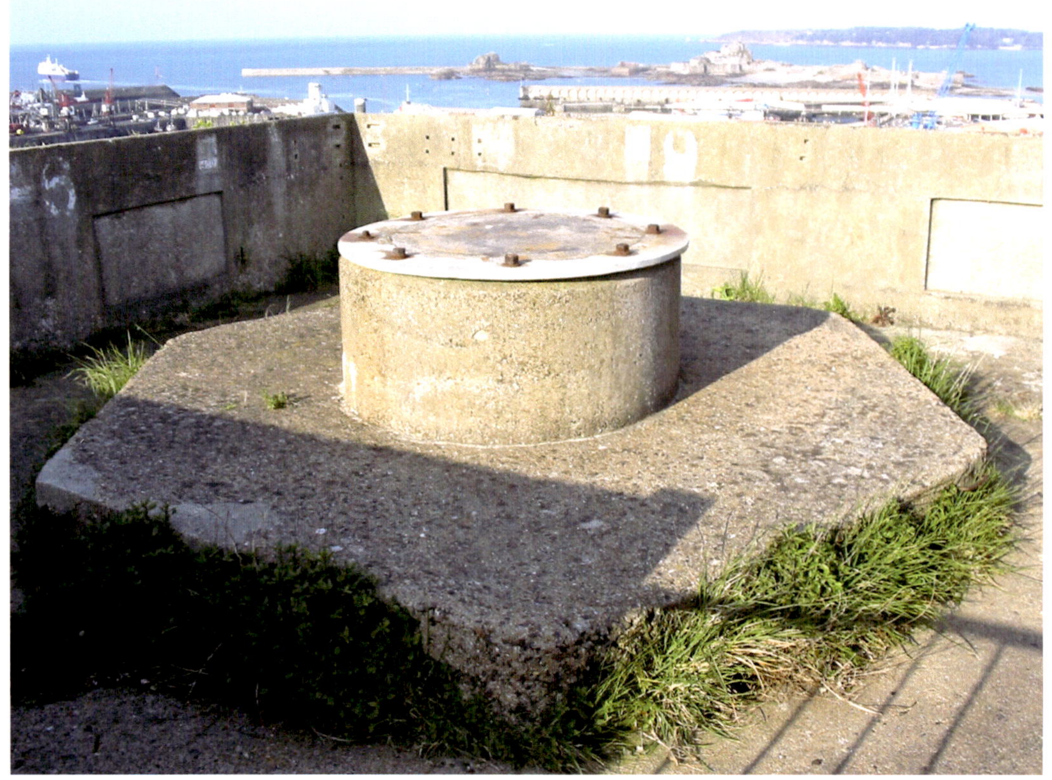

One of the German gun emplacements dating from the occupation. (Public domain)

Fort William

Built in the mid-eighteenth century, this redoubt formed part of the island's defences. Initially known as Prince William's Redoubt, Fort Henry may have been used as a temporary hospital for soldiers wounded in the skirmish at La Rocque at the beginning of the Battle of Jersey in 1781. Square in plan with a surrounding moat, the 4-metre-thick wall offered protection to the men and buildings inside. During the German occupation in the Second World War, it was modified to become Resistance Nest Fort William, complete machine gun positions and shelters. Today, very little remains of the military aspects to Fort William, as a private house was built inside the walls in the years after the conflict.

Grève de Lecq Barracks

Grève de Lecq is one of the few sheltered bays along the North Coast, and in 1779 half of a French Expeditionary Force attempted to land here, forcing the Governor to order the rapid building of a guard house, battery and tower within a year, followed by an additional guard house and battery on the cliff at Le Câtel by 1789. Le Câtel Fort and Battery were soon joined by Middle Battery, Valle du Fort Battery and a Round Tower to protect the bay,

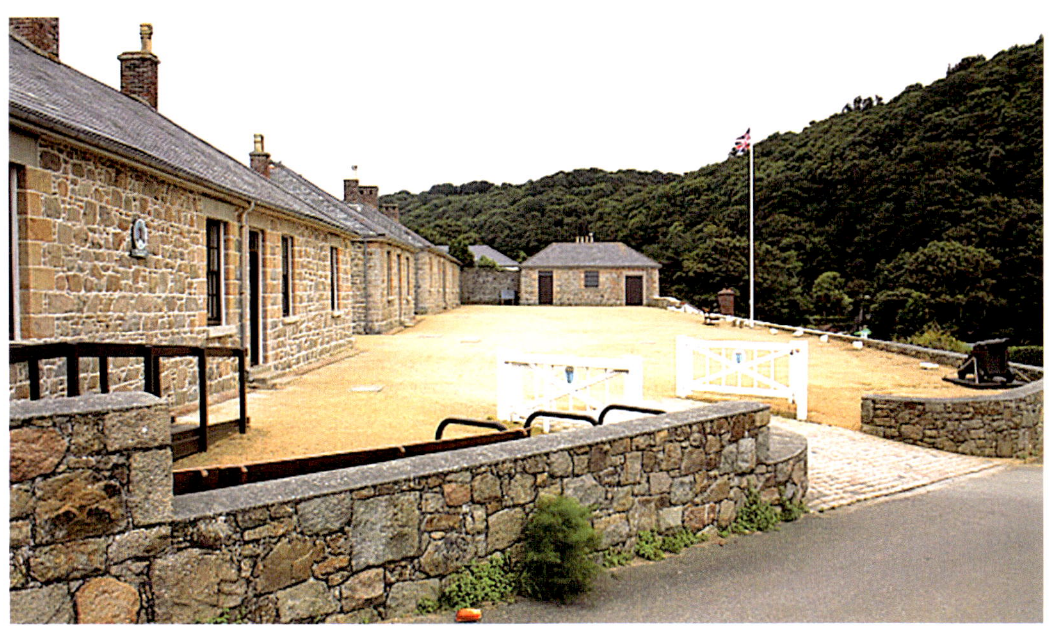

Greve de Lecq Barracks. (Courtesy of Bob Embleton CC BY-SA 2.0)

and as a result, Grève de Lecq Barracks was built in 1810 in order to accommodate the 250 men needed to man the positions. It had two blocks for soldiers, each consisting of four barrack rooms – which would have meant twenty to twenty-five in a room, and two small rooms for non-commissioned officers, who had considerably more space and privacy. The last troops here were withdrawn in 1926 and over the next fifty years or so, the site was left disused. Today it is managed by the National Trust, and it is the only surviving barracks left on the north coast of the Island and retains many original features. As well as the barrack accommodation, which is now a number of holiday lets, surrounding the site are a number of associate buildings, including a coal store, two prison cells and the ablutions block – for those soldiers who had had a bit too much to drink!

Grosnez Castle

There's very little left of Grosnez Castle now, aside from a few walls and an archway, but they give us a tantalising glimpse of what the castle may have looked like when originally built. Protected on three sides by steep cliffs and crashing waves, the fourth landward side had thick high walls, two strong towers and a gatehouse, which allowed access across a dry moat. Likely to have been constructed around the early to mid-fourteenth century on the orders of Sir John des Roches, it was taken by invading French forces in 1373 and 1381. At first sight it is seemingly in a strong defensive position, but the castle had a number of weaknesses – few internal buildings for a garrison to stay in and no fresh water supply being two! These issues led to its quick downfall, and it is thought that it was demolished sometime between 1460 and 1485, having stood for little over a hundred years.

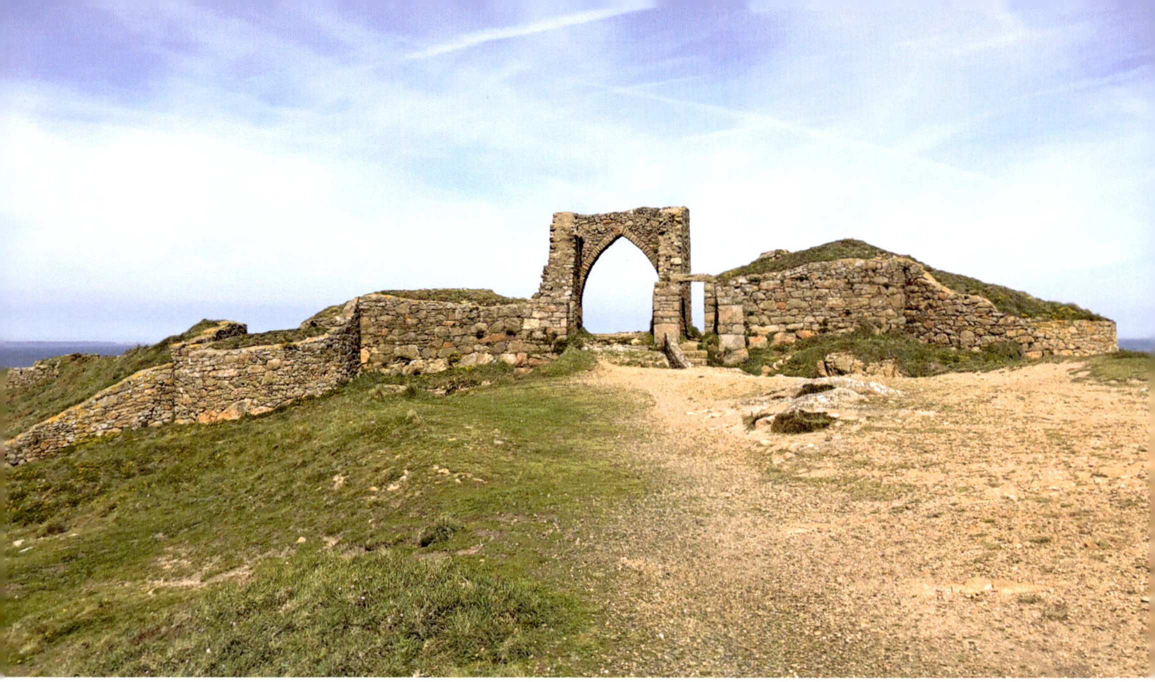

Little now remains of Grosnez Castle. (Author's collection)

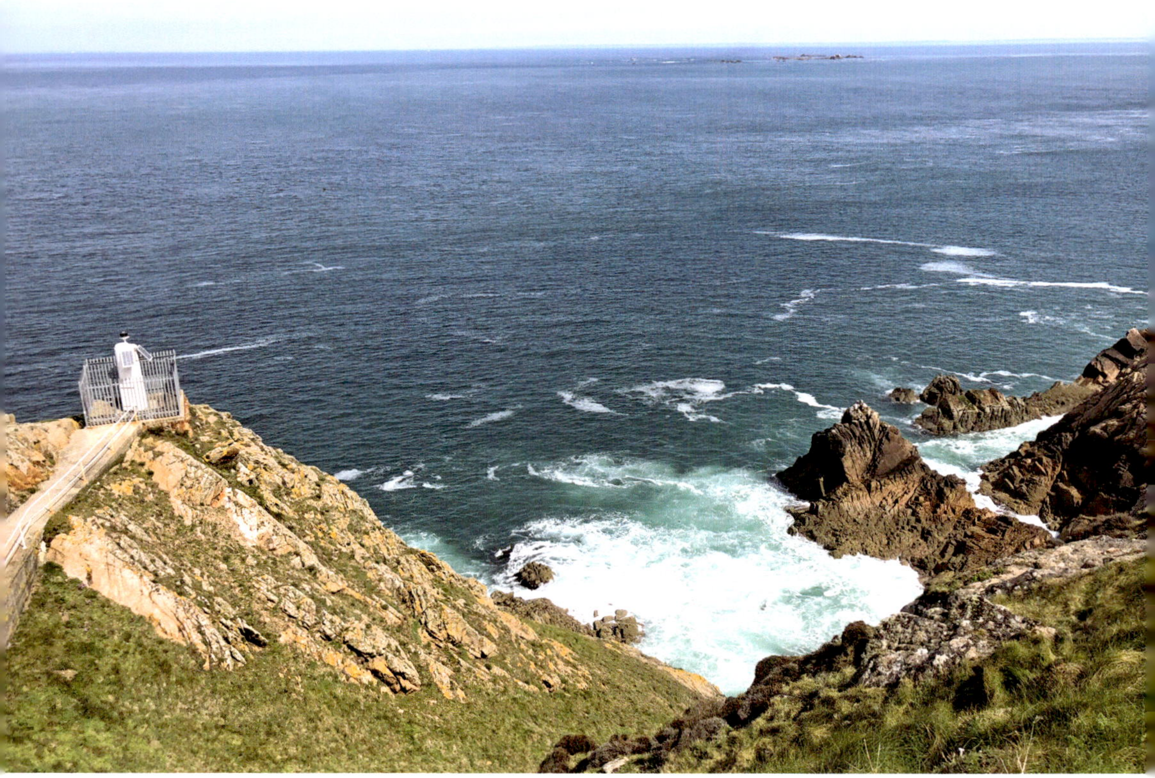

A naval signal station was set up here in 1806. (Author's collection)

Jersey Militia

When England and Normandy 'split' in 1204, there was a need to defend Jersey from the now hostile French. Initially, locally armed men took up this role, but after the exiled King David II of Scotland raided the island from his base in France in 1336, the Warden of the Isles, Thomas de Ferrers, received orders from King Edward III to raise the men of Jersey in readiness for war – and so the Jersey Militia was formed.

When Jersey was invaded by French troops in 1461, the militia were not strong enough to retake Mont Orgueil Castle (which has been surrendered to the French) and it wasn't until a Yorkist English army arrived in 1648 that a nineteen-week siege of the castle finally expelled the invaders – with the St Ouen militia performing with distinction. In 1545, the island's Governor ordered each parish to appoint a captain for its company of twelve trained parochial bands, and this restructuring was put to the test just a few years later in 1549 when French pirates landed at Bouley Bay, with the militia being able to run them back into the sea.

The seventeenth century saw a further restructuring, with the militia being organised into three regiments – West, North and East – and investment in twenty-four artillery cannons. Two were stored in each parish, with a church acting as a muster point for the militia men. The English Civil War came to Jersey in the mid-seventeenth century, and when a Parliamentarian fleet landed at St Ouen's Bay, the militia put up only limited defence, ultimately allowing the Parliamentarians to lay siege to Mont Orgueil and Elizabeth Castle.

In 1730, the militia was divided into five regiments and in 1771 compulsory military service was introduced, with the militia increasing to include a Regiment of Cavalry, a Regiment of Artillery and five Regiments of Infantry.

On 6 January 1781, in what is known as the Battle of Jersey, a French force landed on the east of the island at La Rocque, Grouville ,and marched to St Helier. They surrounded Government House and surprised the island's governor, Major Moses Corbet, taking him prisoner. Despite getting a signed surrender from him, the commander at Elizabeth Castle had other ideas and refused. Command of the island had now passed to the next most senior British commander, twenty-four-year-old Major Francis Peirson, who assembled his men from St Peter's Barracks and the Jersey militia to the west of the town. The troops marched into the town and easily outnumbered the French resulting in their surrender. In 1831, fifty years after this event, the militia received a new title – the Royal Jersey Militia.

In 1837 there were five regiments, with every resident from nineteen to sixty-five expected to bear arms, with sixteen to eighteen year olds being trained weekly. Reorganisation occurred a number of times over the next fifty years, with 1877 seeing the militia having around 280 men in three field gun battalions, coastal defence guns and six purpose-built arsenals constructed across the island.

The 1905 Army Act saw the militia reorganised again to create a regiment of artillery comprising two field and two garrison companies. During the First World War, the militia stayed on the island, aside from one company that was detached to the 7th (Service) Battalion of the Royal Irish Rifles. Some members served as guards at the Blanches Banques Prisoner of War Camp located at St Brélade. A number of men from Jersey did sign up to various British regiments, with 862 being killed during the conflict. What is

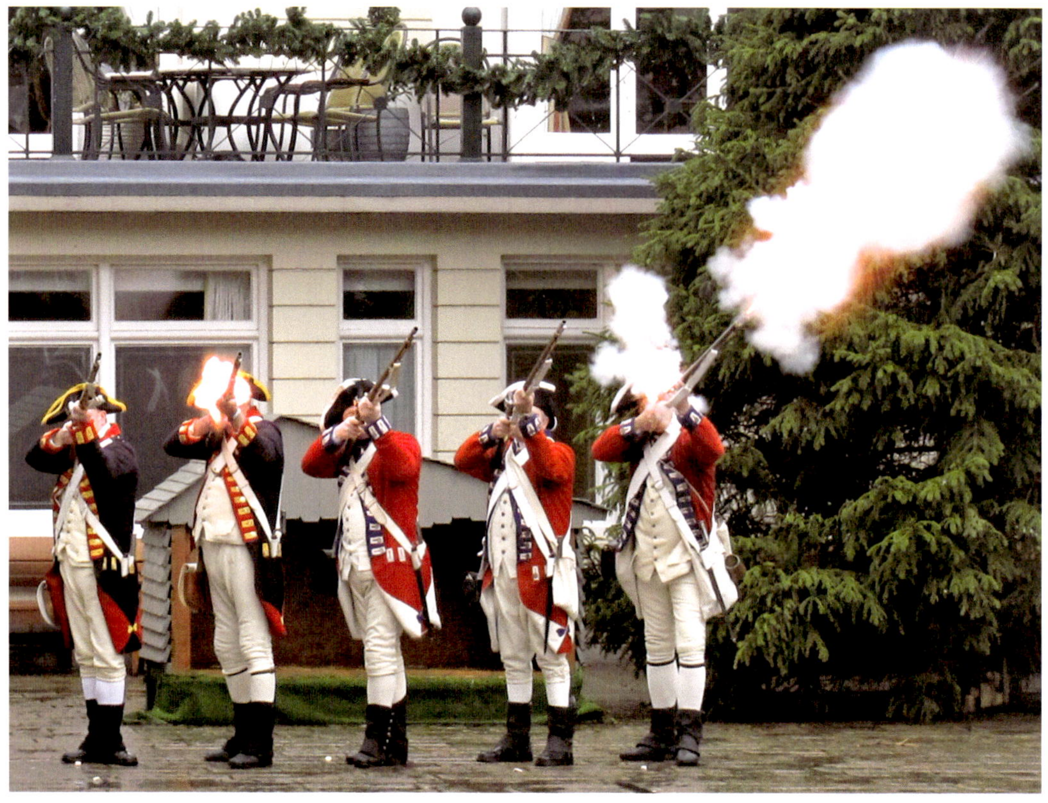

Re-enactors as the Royal Jersey Militia at a Battle of Jersey commemoration in the Royal Square, St Helier. (Courtesy of Man Vyi CC BY-SA 2.0)

often overlooked is the natural links between Jersey and France, with 264 Jersey natives losing their lives whilst serving with the French forces.

When the island was demilitarised, the officers and men of the militia left on 20 June 1940 to form the 11th (Royal Militia Island of Jersey) Battalion, the Hampshire Regiment. After the war, the Jersey Militia were formally disbanded, along with the other British militia regiments, in 1953. In 1987, it was reformed as a Territorial Army regiment.

Jersey War Tunnels

When German forces occupied the island during the Second World War, they decided to construct a vast network of tunnels – using forced and slave workers from nations across Europe – that would allow the safe storage of munitions and food, as well allowing the troops to withstand potential Allied air raids and bombardment. Known as Hohlgangsanlage 8 (abbreviated to Ho8), some of the nearly 1 km of tunnels that go up to 50 metres underground were converted into a casualty clearing station and emergency hospital in late 1943 to early 1944 as it became clear there was likely to be an Allied invasion of Europe. Unfinished tunnels were sealed off and an air conditioning and heating

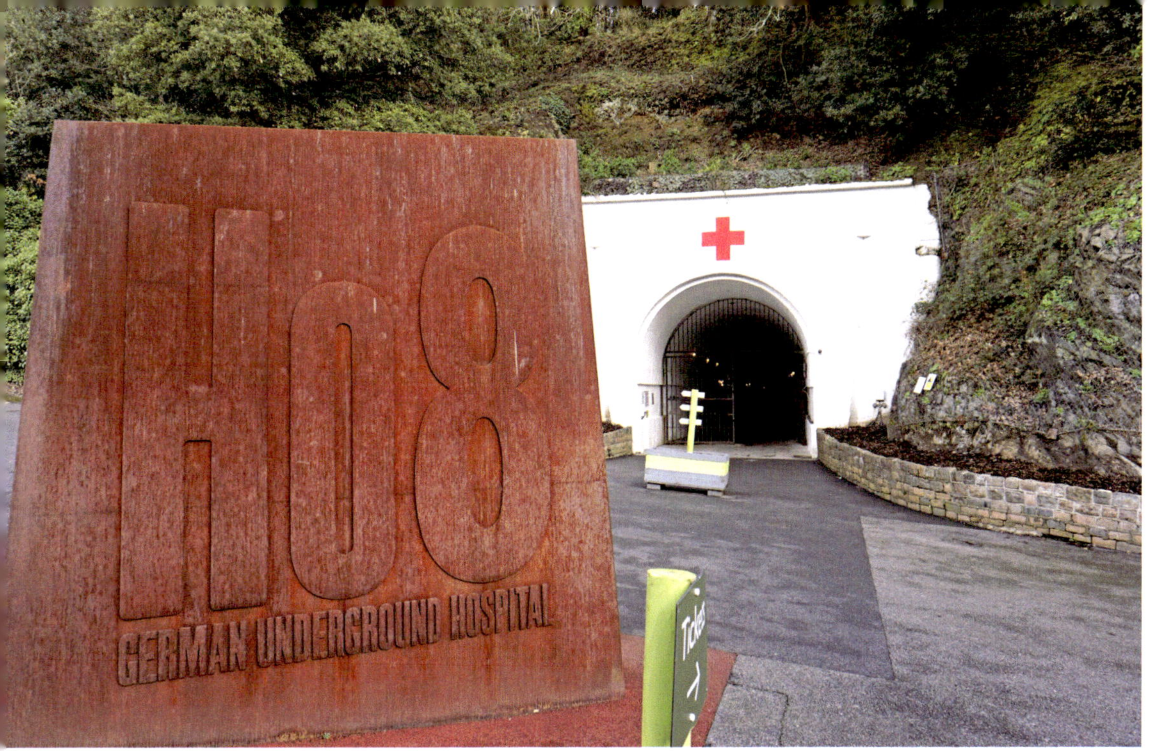

The entrance to the Jersey War Tunnels. (Courtesy of Matt Kieffer CC BY-SA 2.0)

system was installed for the 500-bed hospital – complete with operating theatre. Of course, it was never used as intended. The Allies bypassed the Channel Islands when liberating Europe, and after the war Ho8 fell into disrepair. The tunnels ultimately fell under private ownership, and this saw the complex being restored, with a museum and memorial to the occupation being set up as the German Underground Hospital. Now known as the Jersey War Tunnels, you can visit and experience what life would have been like working in the underground hospital, as well explore the number of different exhibits, focusing on daily life for those on Jersey, cooperation and resistance with the enemy and liberation, amongst others, and there are plenty of artefacts and visual displays throughout.

La Crête Fort

Built on a headland between Bonne Nuit Bay and Giffard Bay, La Crête Fort is a small defensive fort dating from the late eighteenth/early nineteenth century. The review of Jersey's defences in 1778 recommended the creation of a battery at La Crête, and a small two-gun battery was constructed. The small battery has a guardhouse to its rear and would have originally had a ditch surrounding it. In 1834, the fort was improved with a new magazine that would have likely housed two 18-pounder guns and four 12-pounders, as well as a better guardhouse, providing a good base for the thirty or so men that would be stationed here. In 1848, it received an upgrade and housed six 32-pounder cannons – and this is the structure of the fort that remains today. By the end of the nineteenth century

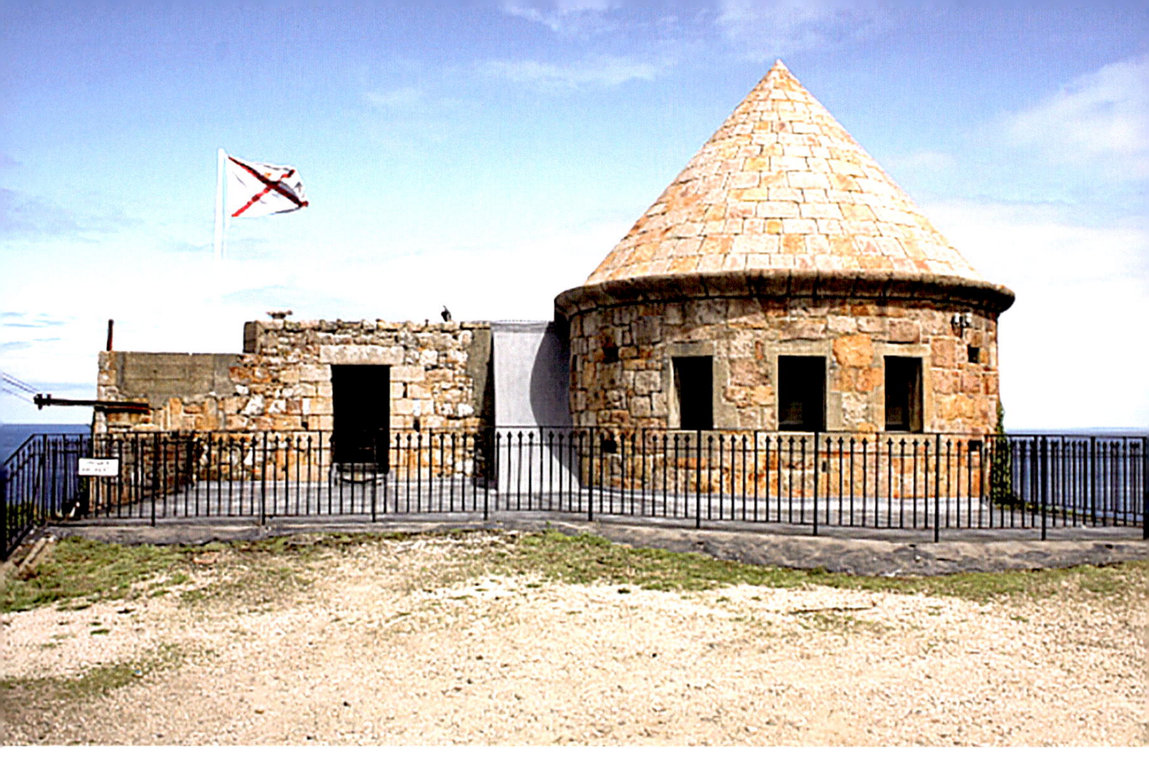

La Crête Fort. (Courtesy of Bob Embleton CC BY-SA 2.0)

it was abandoned, but during the German Occupation of the Second World War, the fort was reinforced and manned by a small contingent of troops. A 3.7 cm PAK anti-tank gun, mortar, several machine guns and a searchlight were installed, although these were never used in anger. Today, La Crête Fort is managed by Jersey Heritage and run as a holiday let.

La Rocco Tower

La Rocco Tower was one of a number of coastal defensive towers built on Jersey to protect the island from a potential French attack. Originally called 'Gordon's Tower' after the Lieutenant-General Andrew Gordon, it was constructed between 1796 and 1801 and its role was to guard St Ouen's Bay from its small offshore tidal island. La Rocco was the twenty-third and last coastal tower in Jersey to be built – it was also the largest and most heavily armed. In 1848, it was recorded as having five 32-pounder guns, but by the end of the nineteenth century it was no longer a useful military site. In 1896, it was included in a list of War Department properties identified as available for disposal, and the States of Jersey purchased the site in 1923 for £100, for the purpose of providing a landmark for shipping. During the Second World War, German forces identified St Ouen's Bay as the most likely point of a potential Allied invasion of Jersey, and they put landmines around the tower, wired to La Braye slipway. In 1943, the accidental detonation of some of these landmines inflicted much damage to the tower, and this wasn't rectified until 1972. Today, it provides an iconic silhouette over St Ouen's Bay.

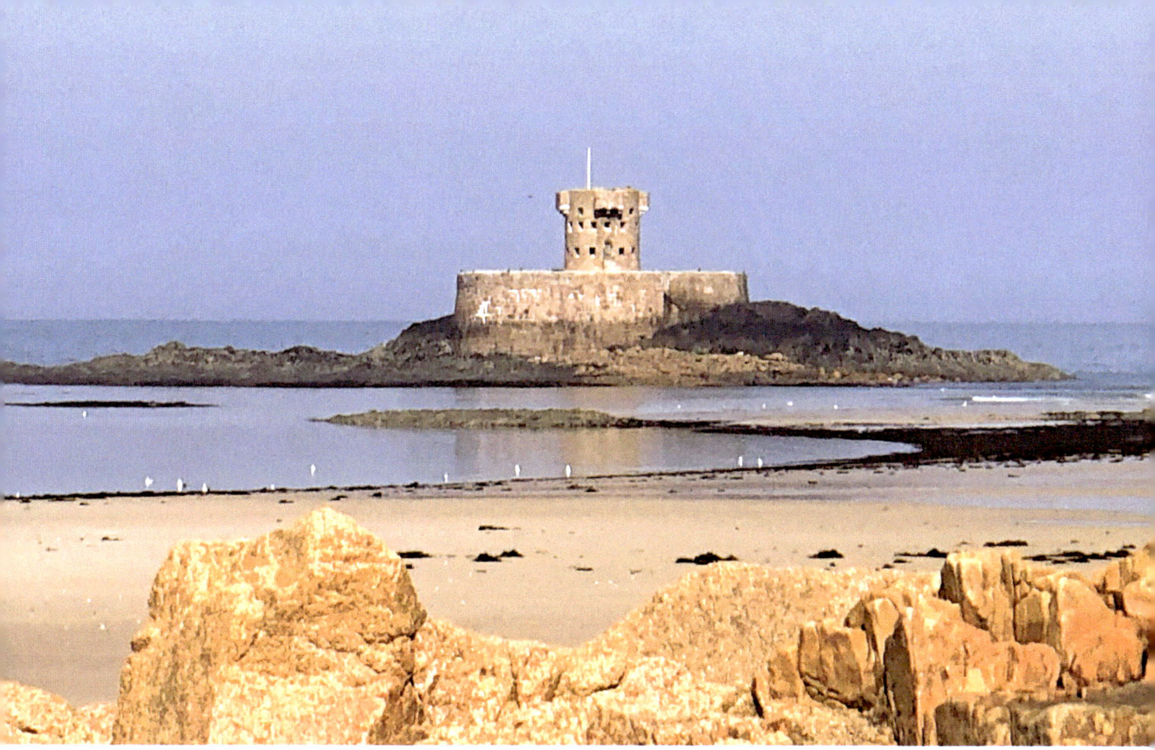

A view of La Rocco Tower from the beach. (Author's collection)

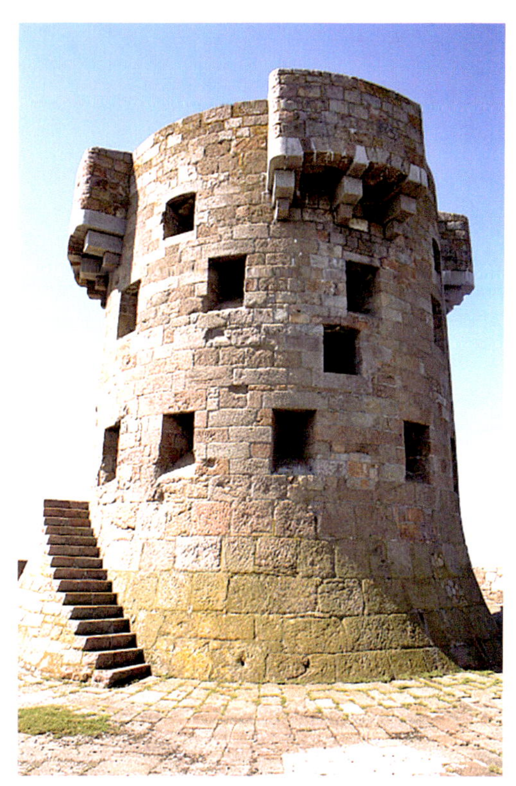

A close-up of La Rocco Tower. (Courtesy of
Bob Embleton CC BY-SA 2.0)

L'etacquerel Fort

L'etacquerel Fort was built on a headland overlooking Bouley Bay in 1836. An earlier battery had been built nearby between 1786 and 1790 – but this was modified by adding a guardhouse and flanking screen walls. Built into the rock itself, its seaward wall is roughly 50 metres above high tide, whilst on the landward side, an impressive twenty-one-foot-deep dry ditch was dug. A small wooden bridge crosses the ditch to an entrance area that contains a guardhouse for a small number of men. The three traversing gun platforms were designed to work in tandem with Fort Leicester to the west, and its isolated position would have made it difficult to take. Now partially ruined, it is maintained by Jersey Heritage.

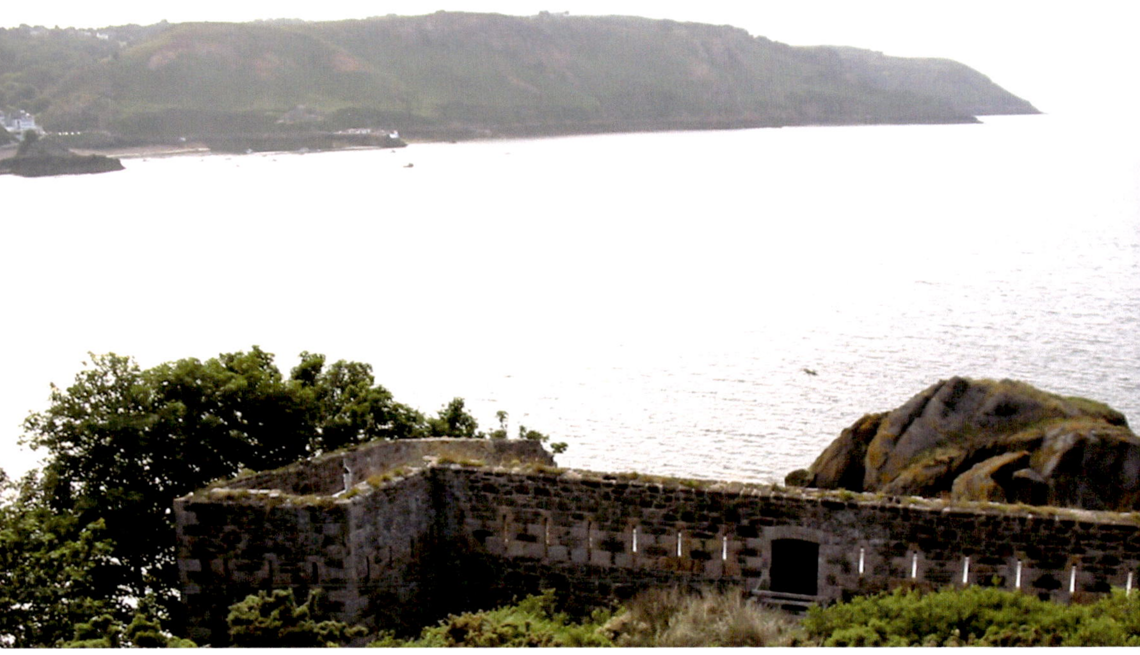

L'etacquerel Fort overlooking Bouley Bay. (Public domain)

Le Câtel Fort and Battery

Le Câtel Fort was built in 1780 as a direct result of half of a French Expeditionary Force attempting to land at Grève de Lecq Bay in 1779. Overlooking Grève de Lecq Bay from its high vantage point, Le Câtel Fort was originally armed with three 32-pounder guns on traversing platforms. Although nearby Grève de Lecq Barracks was designed to provide accommodation for the soldiers, a guardhouse was soon built for the sixteen men required, along with a loop-holed wall, which encircled the position. Today, it occupies a peaceful spot on the North Coast and is run by National Trust Jersey.

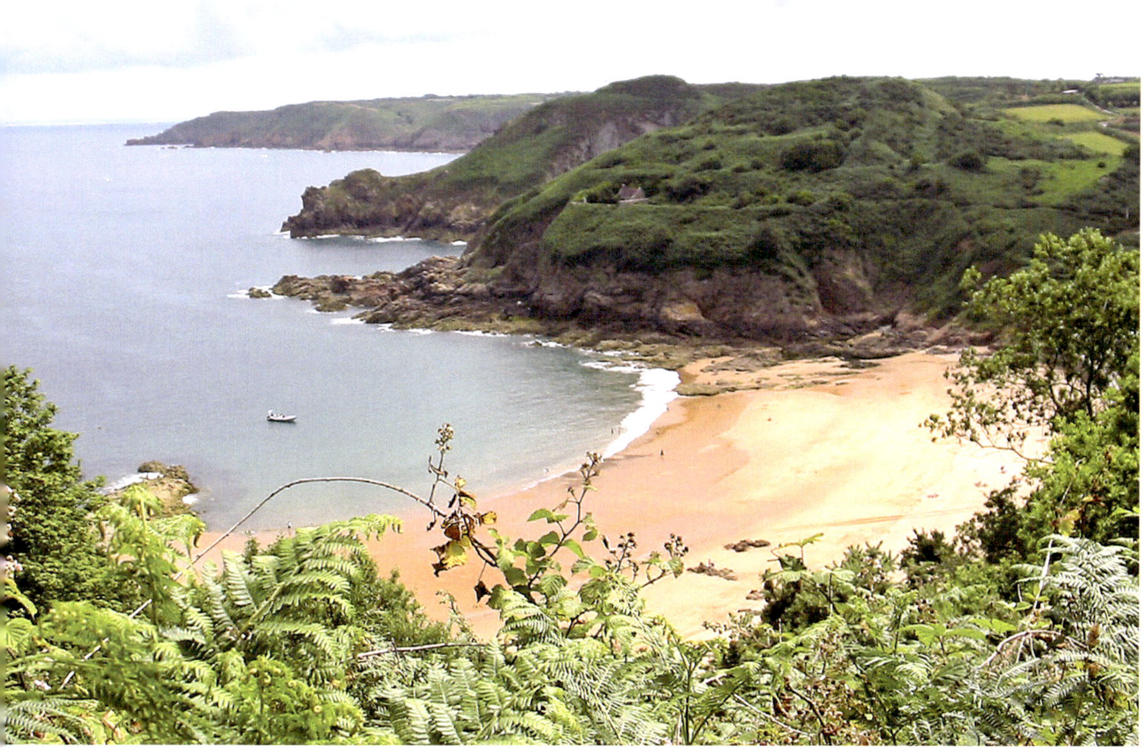

Le Câtel Fort sits nestled into the hillside overlooking Grève de Lecq Bay. (Public domain)

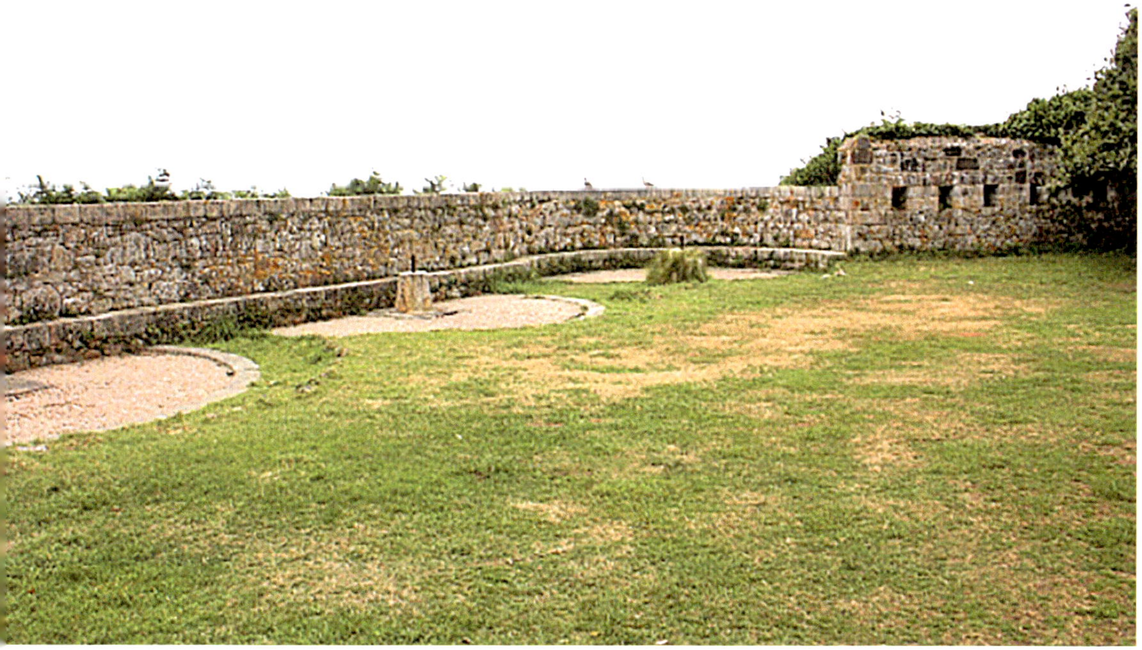

The gun emplacements at Le Câtel Fort. (Courtesy of Bob Embleton CC BY-SA 2.0)

Le Hocq Tower

When the threat of a French invasion seemed imminent in the mid to late eighteenth century, a series of defensive round towers were constructed on the orders of the Governor of Jersey, General Henry Seymour Conway, and Le Hocq is one of these. Likely completed in 1781, the 11-metre-diameter structure was divided up into three levels: the ground floor for storage (including gunpowder) and the other two floors acting as the living quarters for the ten men who were stationed here. There would have been an 18-pounder carronade on a wooden traversing platform mounted on the roof, with another two or three 18-pounder cannons next to the tower on a small-paved area. Although it fell into disuse by the beginning of the twentieth century, the Germans occupying the island during the Second World War did replace the wooden floors with concrete ones in order to strengthen the tower, and they manned it for the duration of the conflict. Today, Le Hocq Tower has a rather distinctive white patch painted on its seaward side to act as a daymark for shipping navigation.

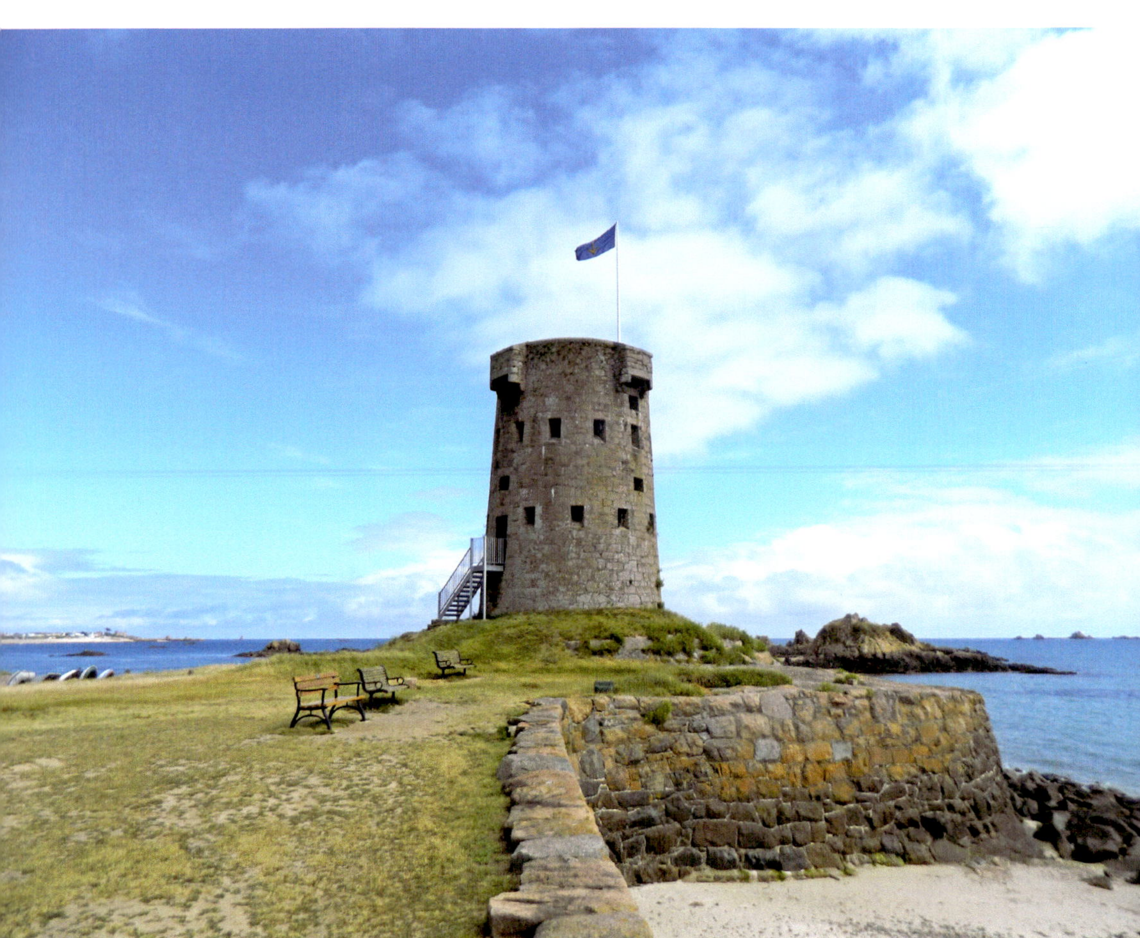

Le Hocq Tower. (Courtesy of Ruben Holthuijsen CC BY 2.0)

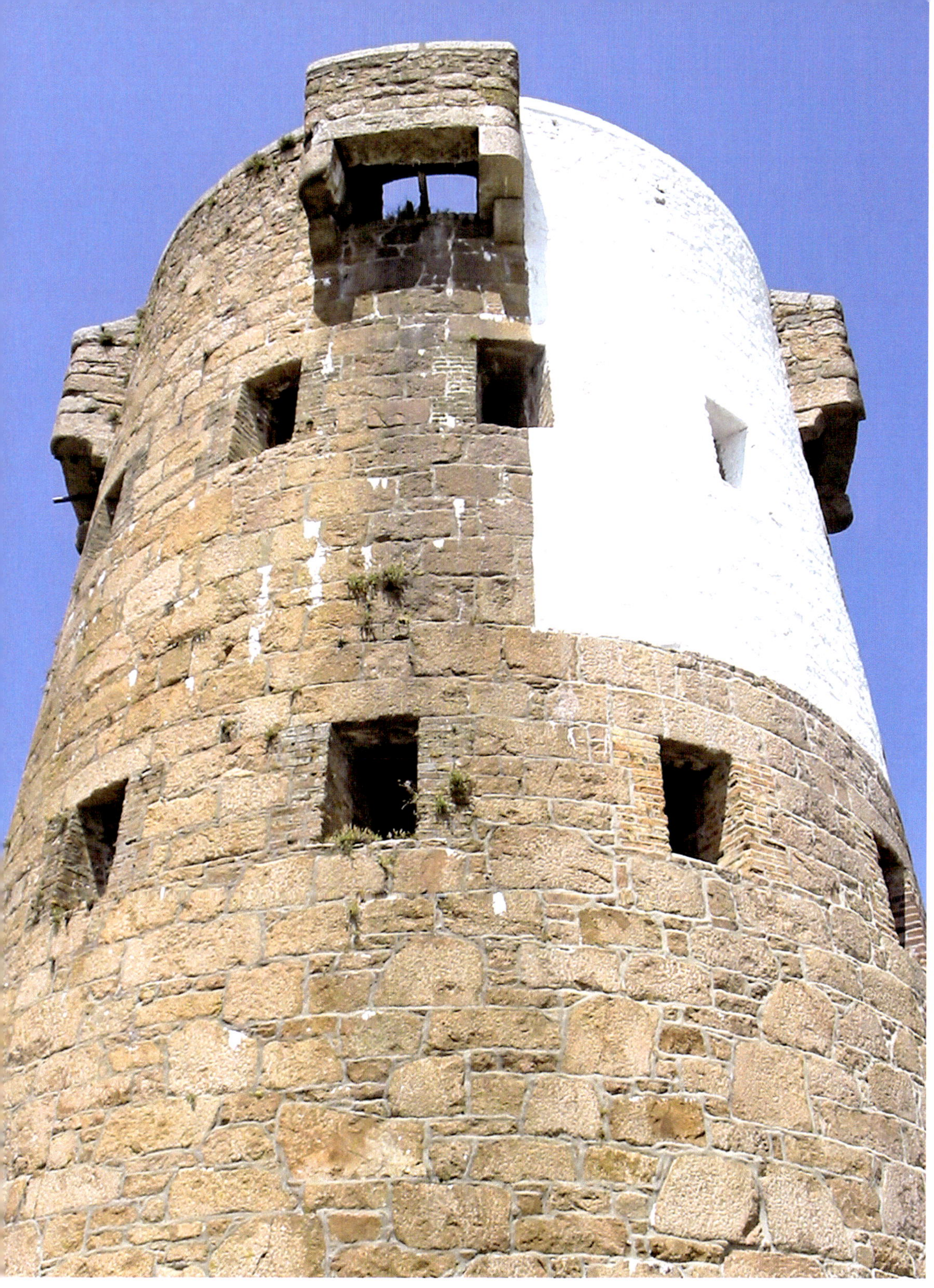

The distinctive white patch painted on the seaward side of Le Hocq Tower. (Public domain)

Mont Orgueil Castle

Sat overlooking Gorey harbour on the east of Jersey, Mont Orgueil was originally constructed between 1204 and 1212 as the islands chose to remain loyal to the Norman duke, John (who was also the King of England), as a power struggle with the French king, Philip II Augustus, loomed on the horizon. Built on a rocky ridge, which was the site of an old Iron Age hill fort, it was a large undertaking, and the ramparts and towers were soon strengthened in 1224.

Over the next 400 years the castle was subjected to a number of attacks by French forces, and being the main fortress in Jersey, it went through a number of improvements and developments. In July 1373, the Constable of France, Bertrand du Guesclin, attacked the castle with an estimated force of 2,000 men. By concentrating his firepower on one part of the castle, he managed to breach the Outer Ward walls. However, the garrison retreated to the inner parts of the castle, which the French could not breach, and the fighting continued until a relief force from England arrived. Although the castle itself was strong, and protected Gorey harbour well, other parts of the island were less secure, and the French continued to raid the island – as demonstrated in 1403.

Also known as Gorey Castle, it was 'taken' by the French in 1461, although it was more of a transfer of power as Margaret of Anjou, the French-born wife of Henry VI of England, seemingly handed control of the island over in return for French aid and assistance during the Wars of the Roses. This didn't last long, however, as the castle was retaken in 1468 by a force led by Sir Richard Harliston.

The development of cannon warfare led to much needed renovation taking place, as the castle would be susceptible from landward attack – particularly from the hill to the west. Platforms for artillery were built in 1548 and 1549; the keep was extended into a D-shaped bastion in 1551, which was better against artillery fire; and a large L-shaped Grand Battery, facing west, was constructed in 1560. However, by 1600, Elizabeth Castle was now the primary defensive position on Jersey and Walter Raleigh moved the Governor's official place of residence from Mont Orgueil to the new castle.

The castle was used as a prison in the 1600s and during the English Civil War, it was from Mont Orgueil that the Royalists under Sir George Carteret, retook the island from the Parliamentarian forces in November 1643. By the end of the seventeenth century the castle was in a ruinous state, and it wasn't until 1730–1734 that some repairs were carried out. In the 1790s, the castle became the base for a French anti-revolutionary spy network named La Correspondance, and aside from housing a few troops over the years, this was the end of the castle's military life. It was formally handed to the people of Jersey in 1907 as an historic monument.

That was, until the German Occupation in the Second World War. They recognised the potential strategic location of Mont Orgueil, using rooms in the keep as a barracks and adding observation towers, trenches and gun positions, although they were never used in anger.

The castle is split into four sections: the Outer Ward, Lower Ward, Middle Ward and the Keep.

The Outer Ward was a very large, enclosed area that was dominated by the curtain walls of the castle overlooking it. It was through this Outer Ward that anyone wishing to enter the castle would need to go through. The First Gate, which has the remains of the original thirteenth-century gate a few metres behind it, has the 1470 built Harliston Tower beside it.

Passing through the Outer Ward you finally reach the Second Gate, the entrance point to the Lower Ward. Built as a tower, before being turned into a gate, the room above it was used as a prison in the seventeenth and eighteenth centuries. The Lower Ward contained a number of associated buildings for the running of the castle, before a number of them were cleared around 1800 to make a large parade ground. With Helie's Tower and the Southern Tower overlooking the harbour and the Cornish Bastion built into the curtain wall in 1547, this was a well defended area.

The route to the Keep winds its way through Queen Elizabeth Gate and into the Middle Ward, which has seen much redesign and redevelopment over the years. The Grand Battery was built here and there are the remains of the old chapel and a long cellar for storage. All of this within the shadow of the Keep, and the more recent residential apartments. The Mount Gate offered those is the Keep, a final chance to keep invaders out – if they ever got that far – and beyond lay the Medieval Great Hall, the Undercroft and a number of towers that can see for miles around.

Jersey has a rich history and Mont Orgueil has overseen it all!

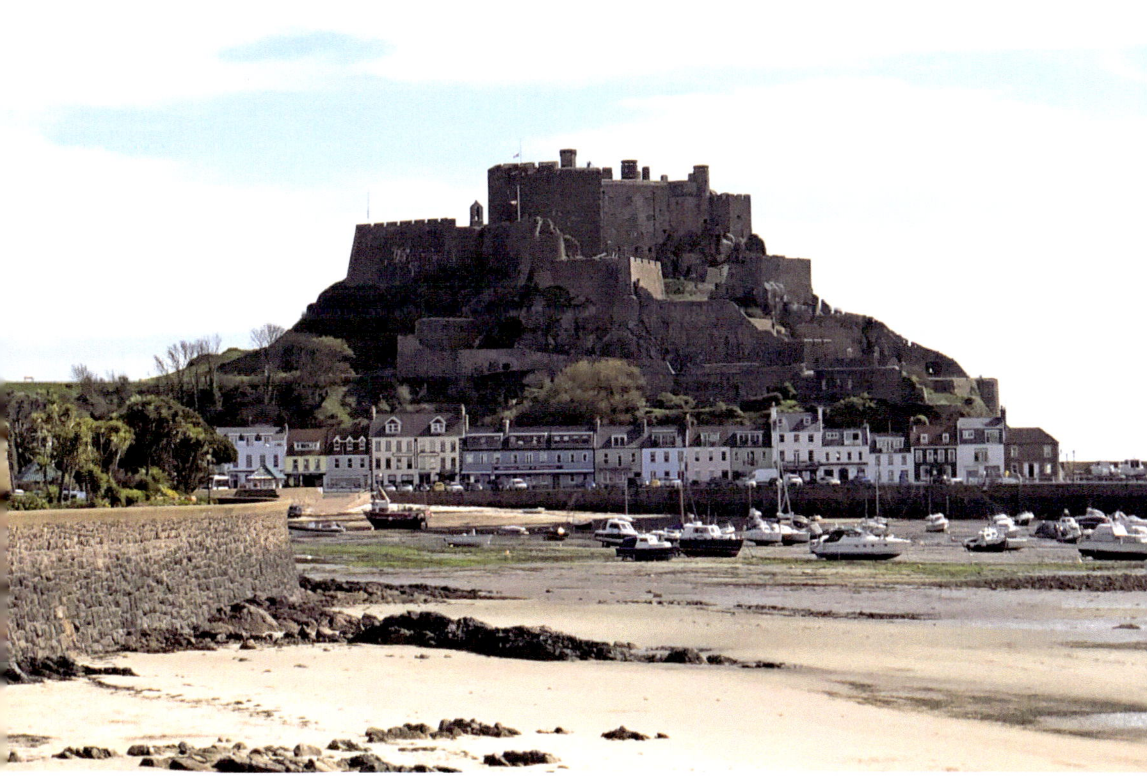

Mont Orgueil sitting above Gorey harbour. (Author's collection)

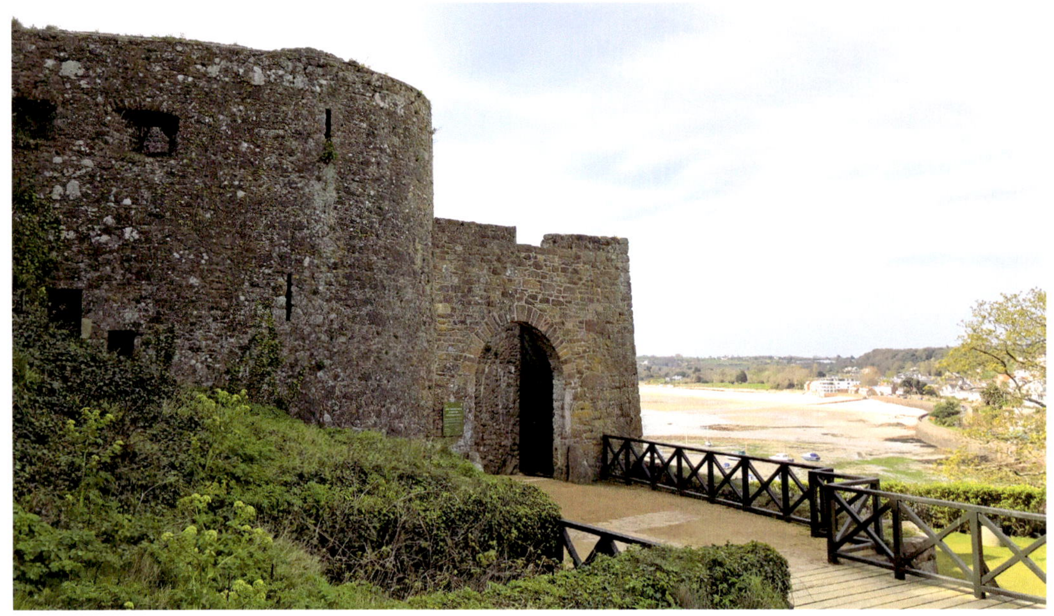

Harliston Tower and the First Gate to the castle. (Author's collection)

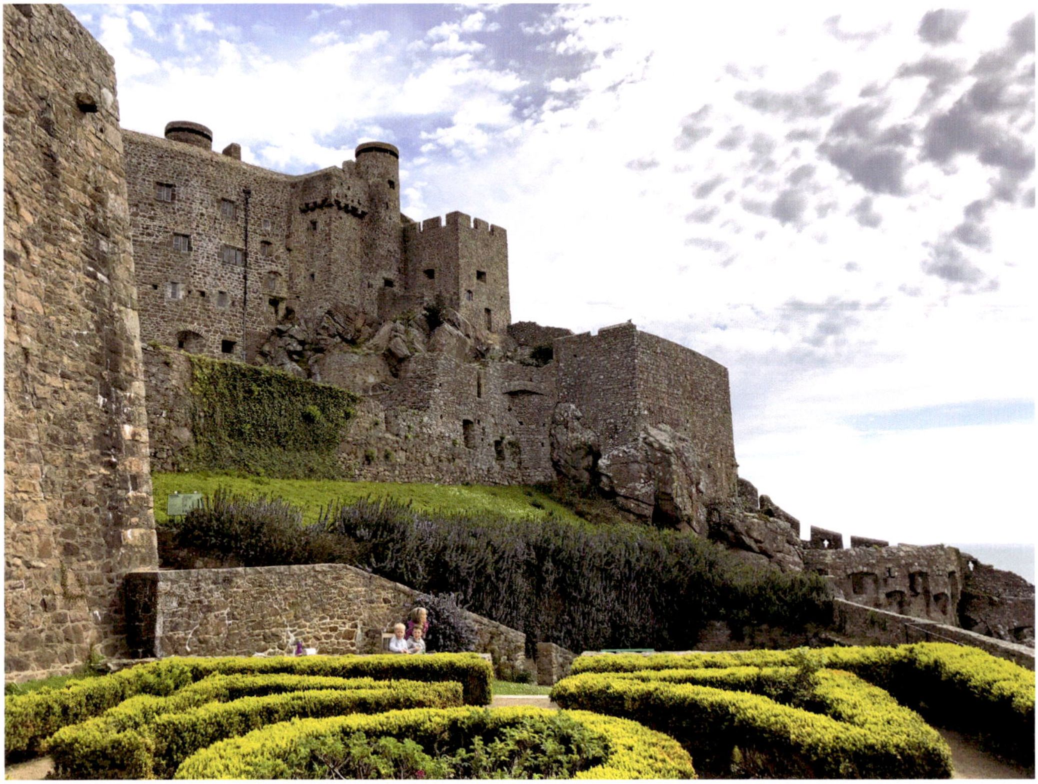

A view of the Tudor Residential Apartments from the De Carteret Garden. (Author's collection)

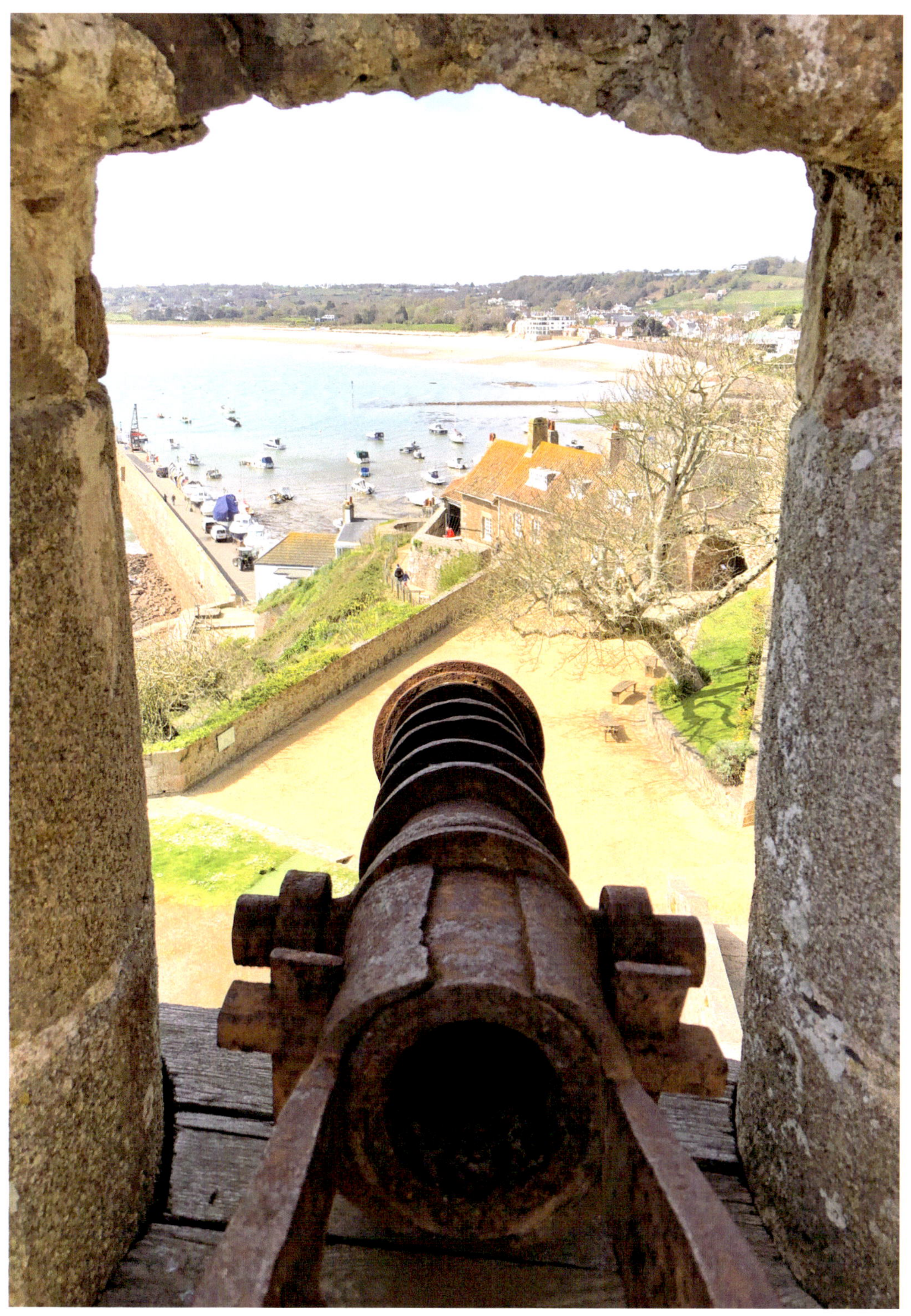

A cannon in the Cornish Bastion overlooks the Second Gate. (Author's collection)

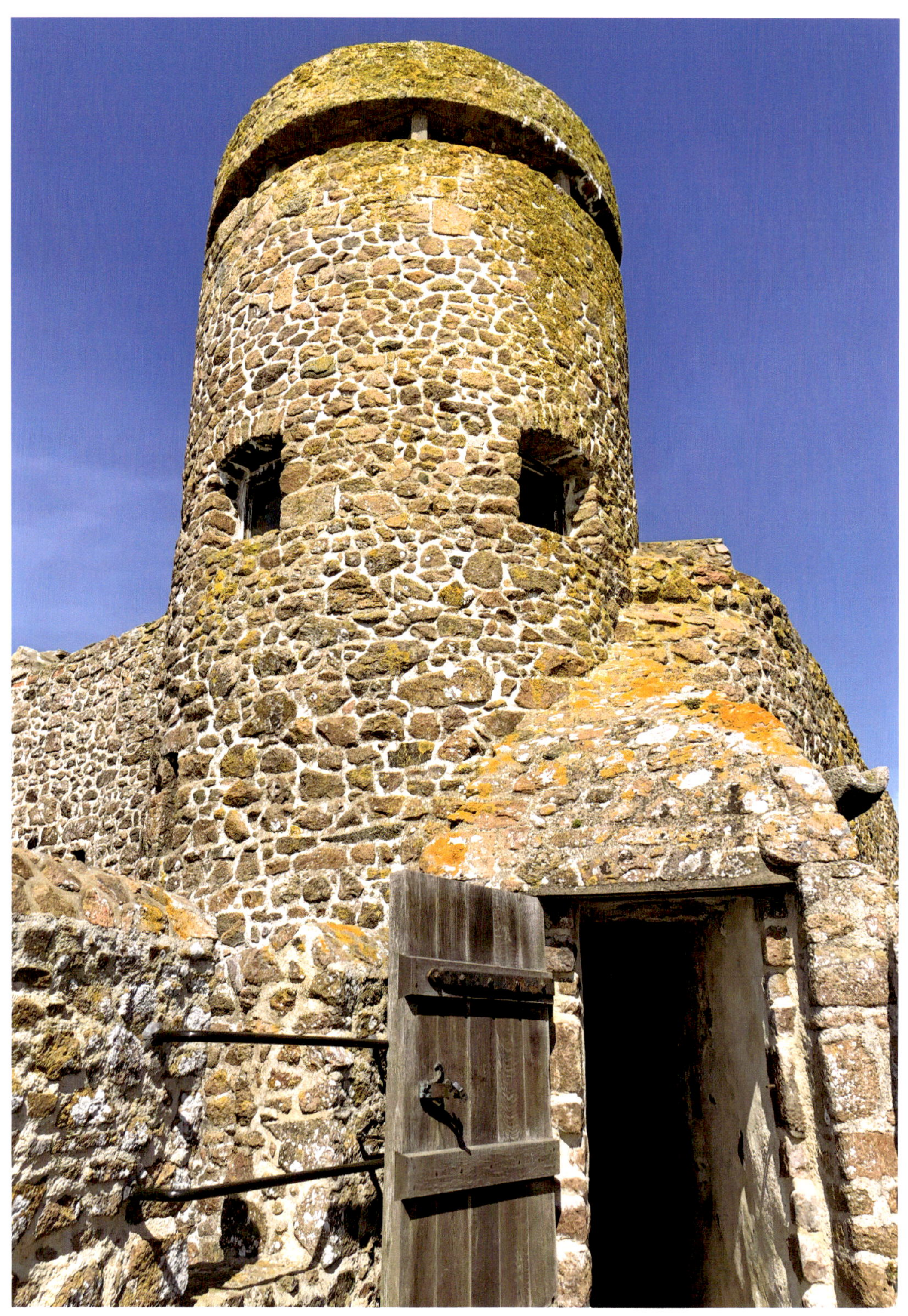

A German Second World War observation point at the top of Mont Orgueil. (Author's collection)

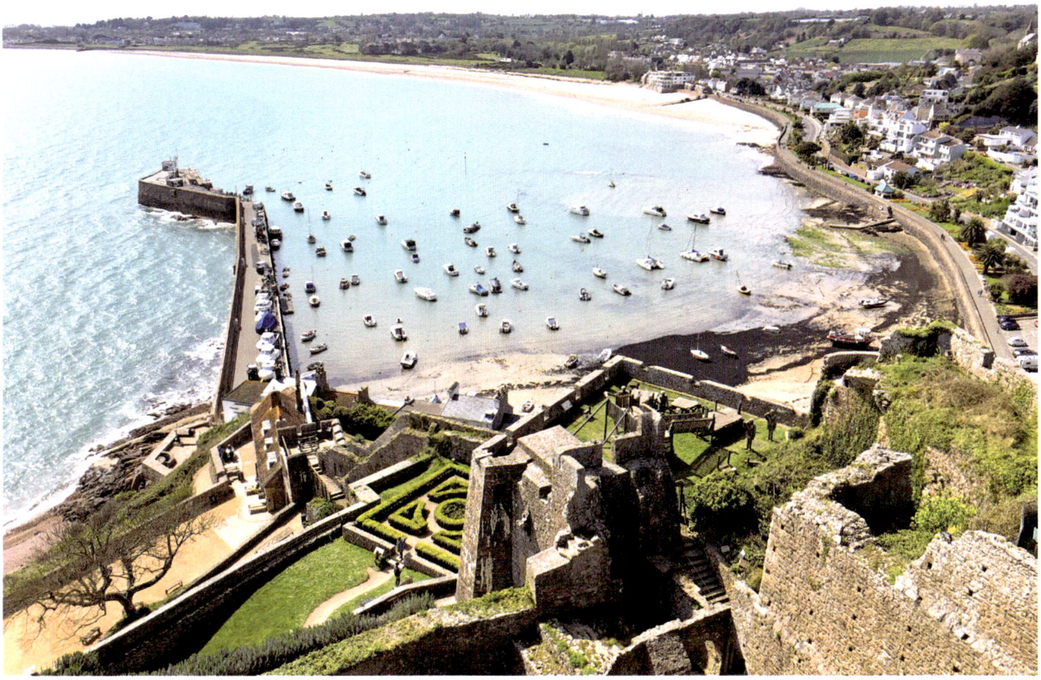

A view of Gorey harbour from the Gundeck at the very top of the castle. (Author's collection)

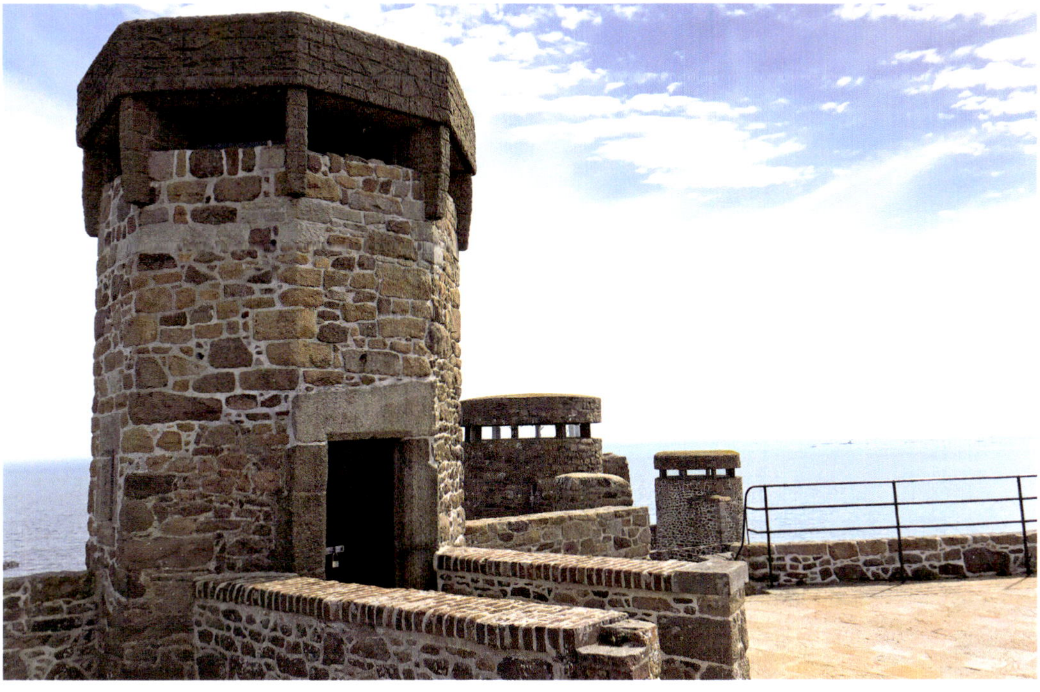

The octagonal turret on Mount Battery was used as an observation post during the German occupation. (Author's collection)

Resistance Nest, Millbrook

Located on Victoria Avenue, opposite the Old Station Café at Millbrook, it is an excellent 4.7 cm anti-tank gun casemate. Built into the sea wall by the German occupying forces of the Second World War, a small group of around ten would have occupied this site with the aim of stopping any Allies landing on the vast stretch of sand. Armed with a light machine gun and one 4.7 cm Czechoslovakian anti-tank gun, this resistance nest is similar to many built right across the island. What sets it apart from the others is the fact that it was sealed up after the war and only reopened in 1985. The CIOS have restored it to a wonderful condition, with a vast number of original items inside.

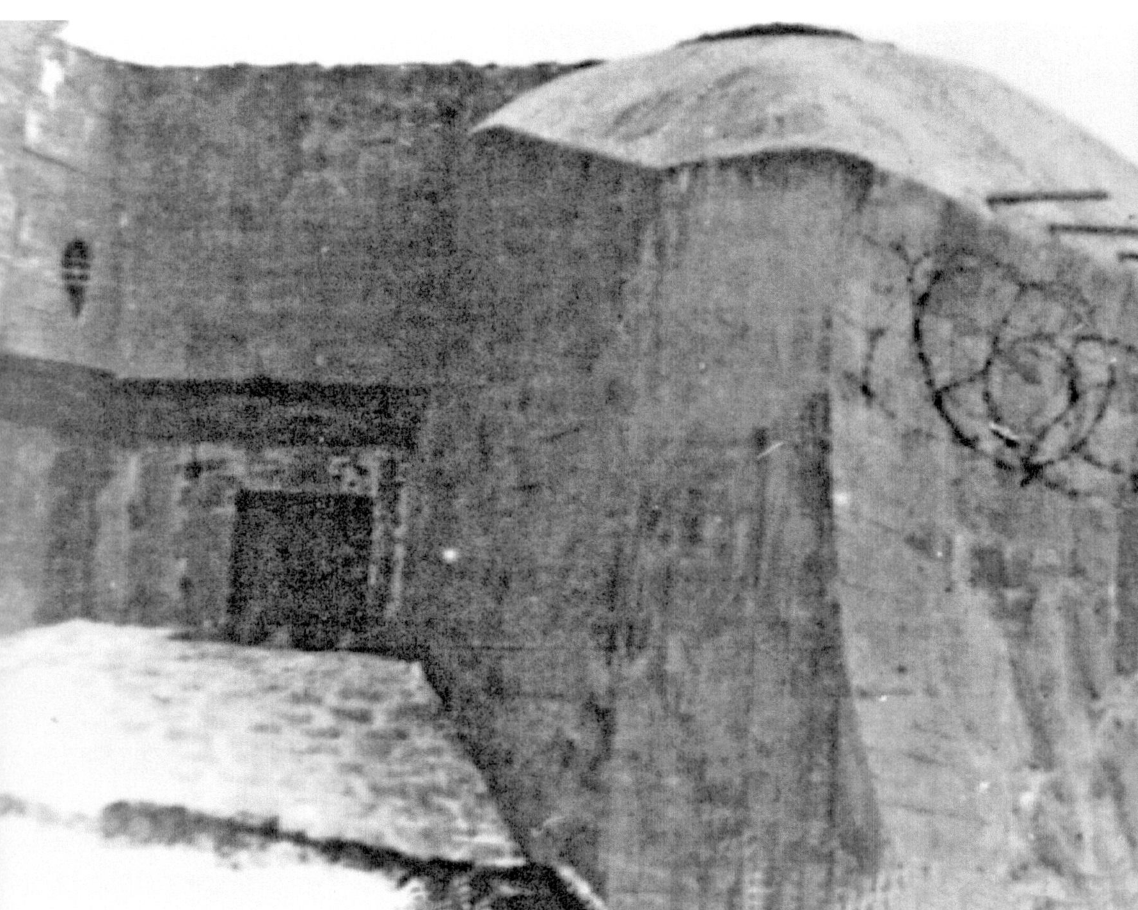

Widerstandsnest (Resistance Nest) Millbrook during the occupation. (Courtesy of the Channel Island Occupation Society (Jersey))

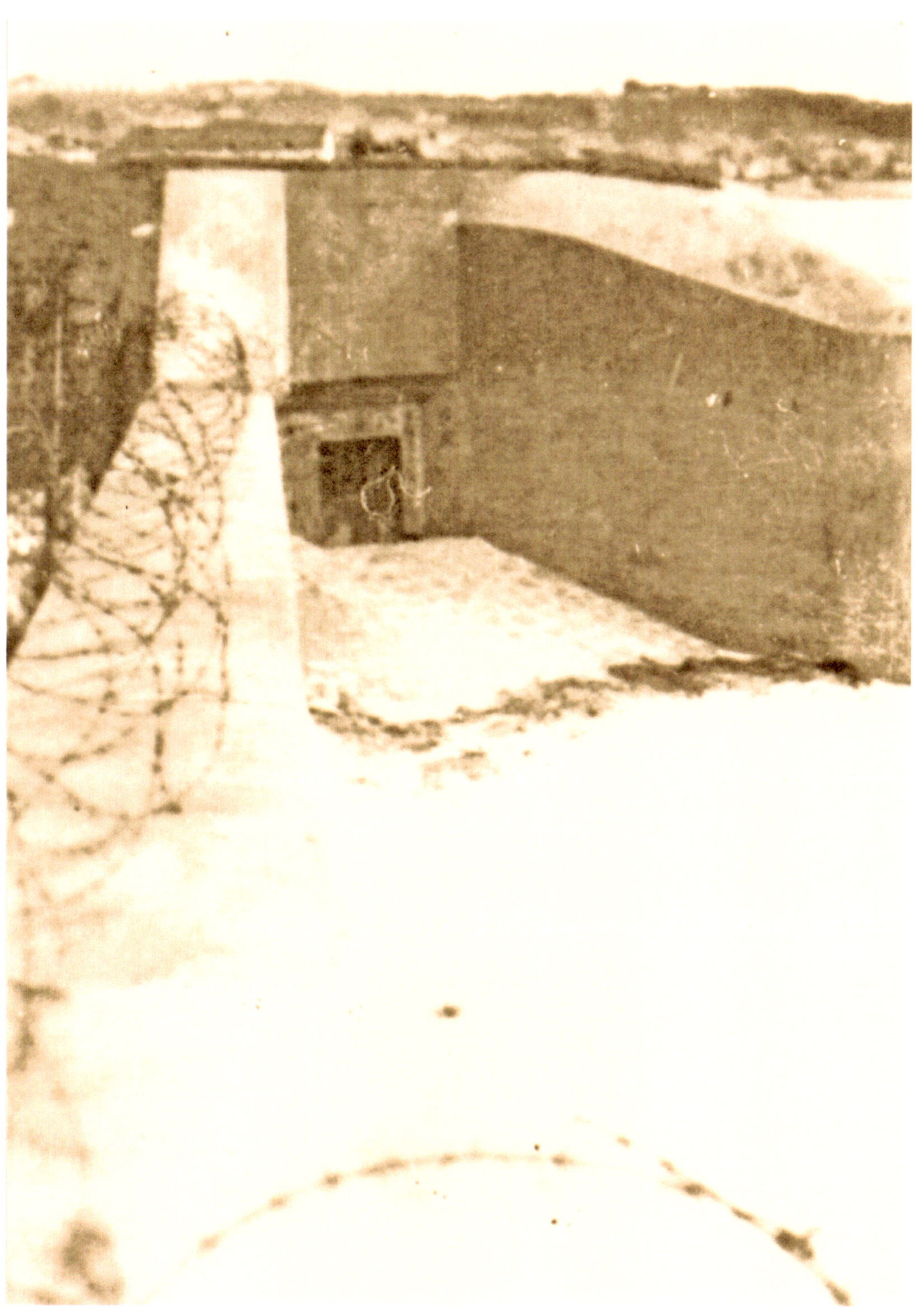

The Resistance Nest during the occupation, with barbed wire along the sea wall. (Courtesy of the Channel Island Occupation Society (Jersey))

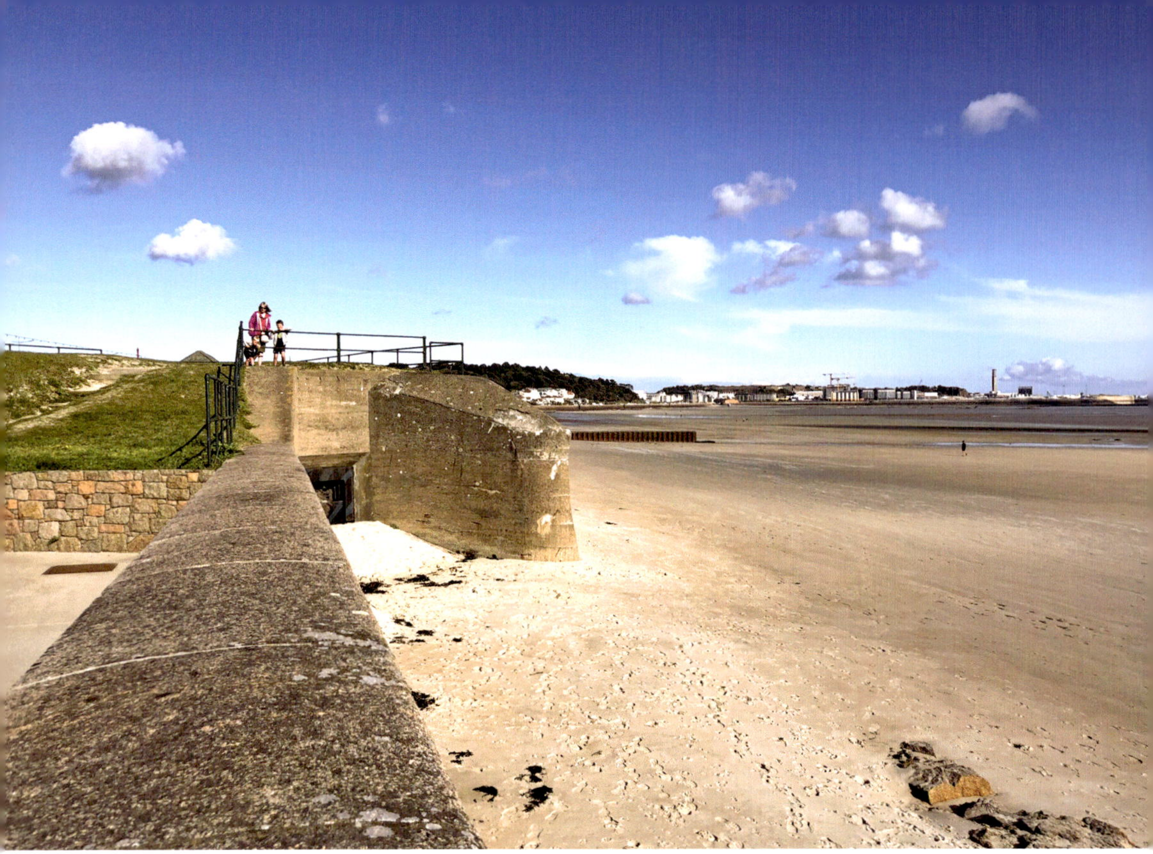

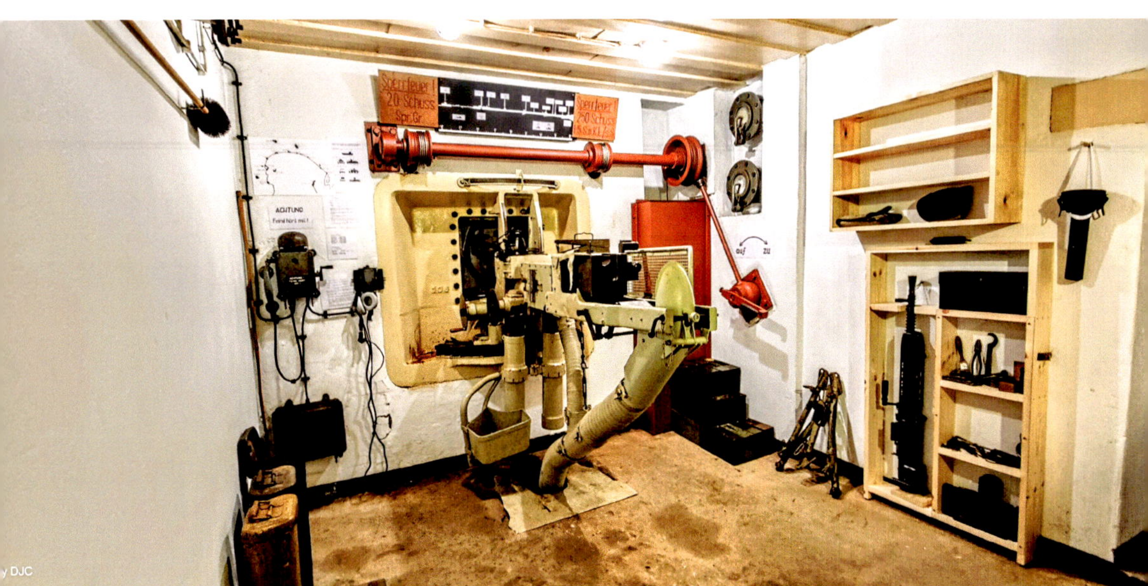

A view of Millbrook today. (Author's collection)

The 4.7 cm Czech anti-tank gun inside the bunker. (Courtesy of the Channel Island Occupation Society (Jersey))

Seymour Tower

Built on a rocky outcrop a few miles from the south-east coast of the island in 1782, Seymour Tower was one of the 'Conway' towers that were constructed to protect Jersey from future French attack. Instead of the usual round design, Seymour Tower is a square tower made from Jersey granite and it had its main gun battery at its base as opposed to on its roof. The tower was able to command the entrance to Grouville Bay and the approach to Mont Orgueil Castle and regular signals were sent back every half hour to indicate if all was well. By the mid to late nineteenth century, Seymour Tower was abandoned in favour of long-range guns being installed at La Rocque point. Since 2006 it has been in the hands of Jersey Heritage.

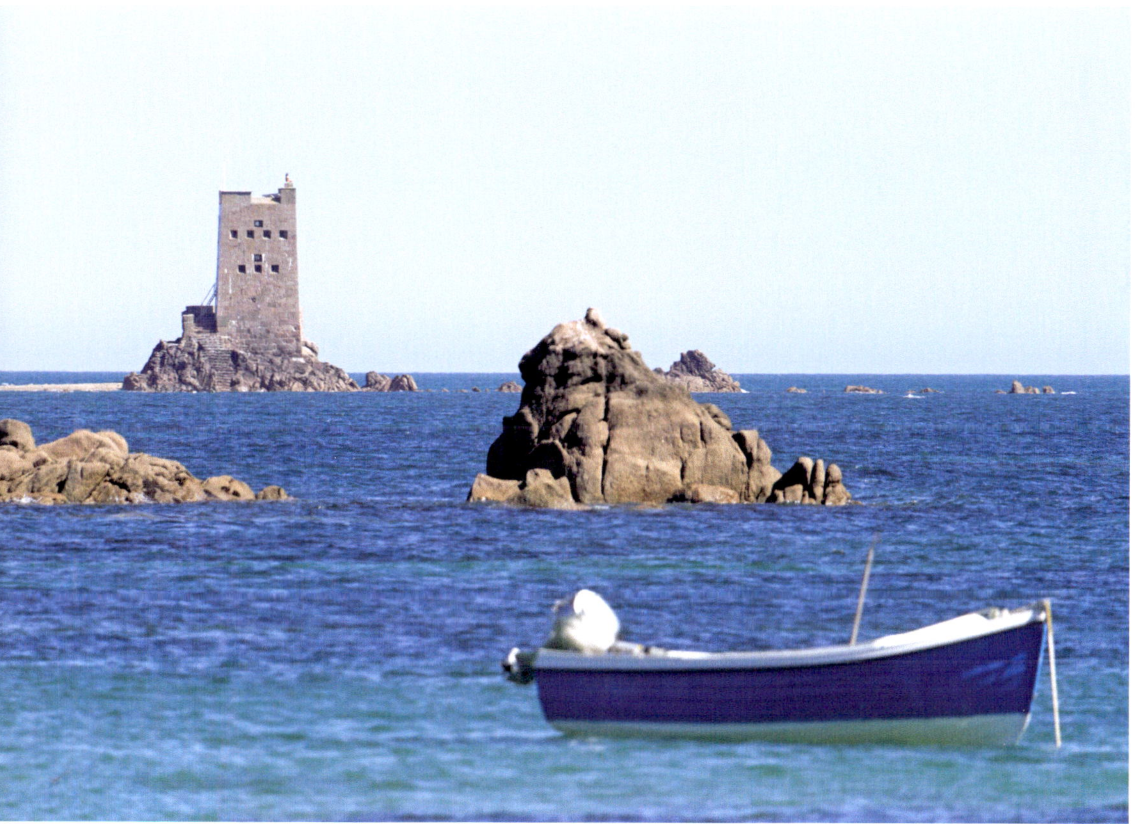

Seymour Tower. (Courtesy of Dan Rok CC BY-SA 3.0)

St Aubin's

When ships unloaded their cargo at St Aubin's Harbour, they were vulnerable to attack by French pirates coming into the bay. As a result, it was decided to build a tower on a rocky offshore island in the 1540s to house four guns and this was named St Aubin's Fort. During the Civil War, the Parliamentarians strengthened the site, and once the Royalists had regained control, they replaced the new earthworks with granite ramparts. The fort was redesigned in both the eighteenth and nineteenth centuries, and during the Second World War, German occupying forces strengthened the fort for their own defensive purposes by adding concrete casemates and guns.

When Hitler ordered the Channel Islands to be made into an impregnable fortress in 1941, additional bunkers and defensive positions were constructed right across Jersey and it is no surprise that the nearly 3 miles of flat sandy beach and numerous slipways along St Aubin's Bay received special treatment. Worried that Allied landing craft might try to land here, the slipways were blocked off or destroyed, bunkers were built at regular intervals, and miles of anti-tank walls, obstacles and barbed wire were put in place. The defences stretched from Elizabeth Castle right the way round to St Aubin's Harbour and it is possible to walk the entire length of the esplanade, seeing the vast majority still in situ today.

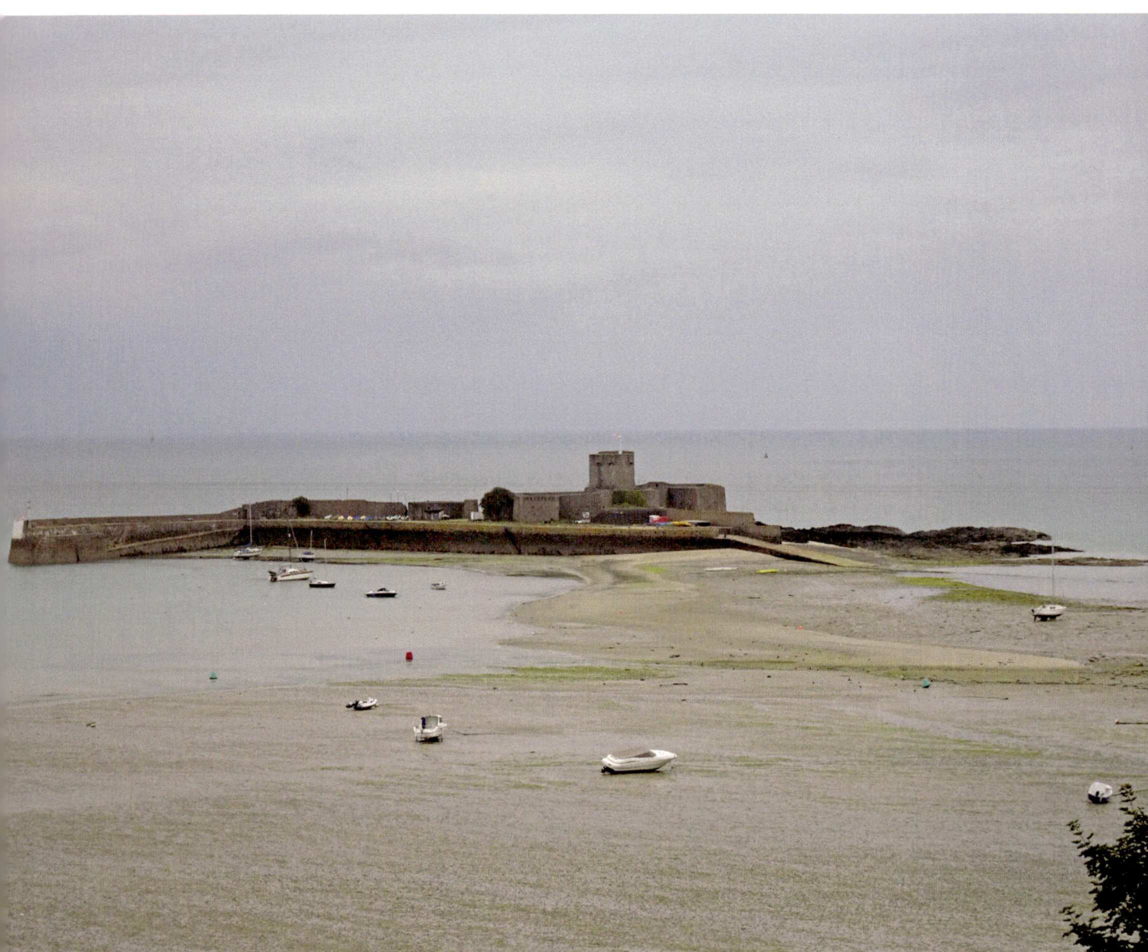

St Aubin's Fort. (Courtesy of Hugh Llewelyn CC BY-SA 2.0)

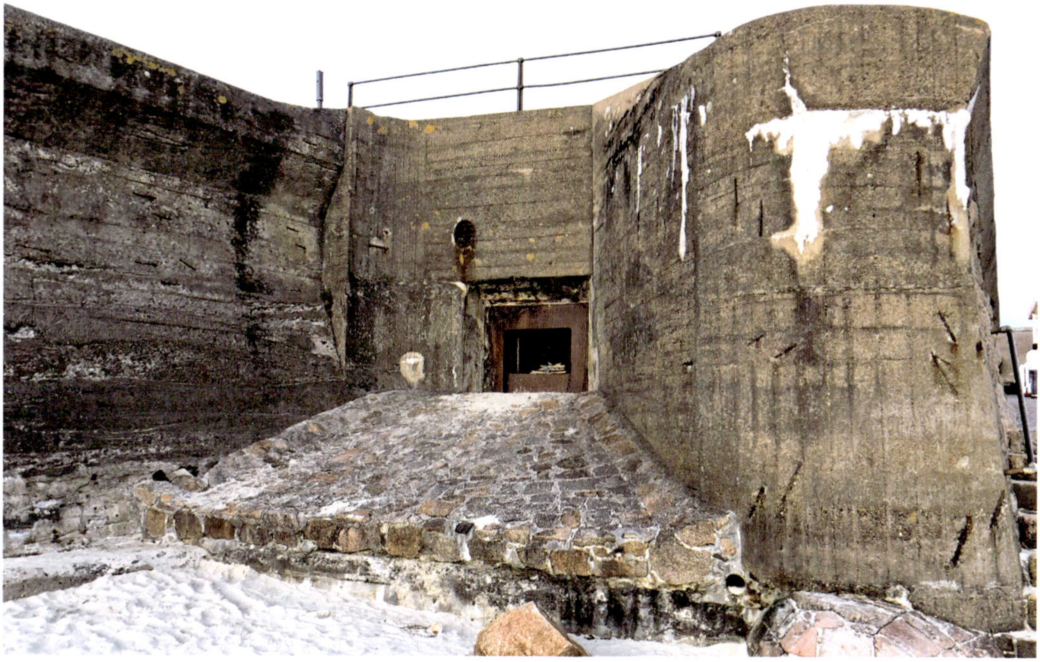

The Bel Royal casemate bunker. (Author's collection)

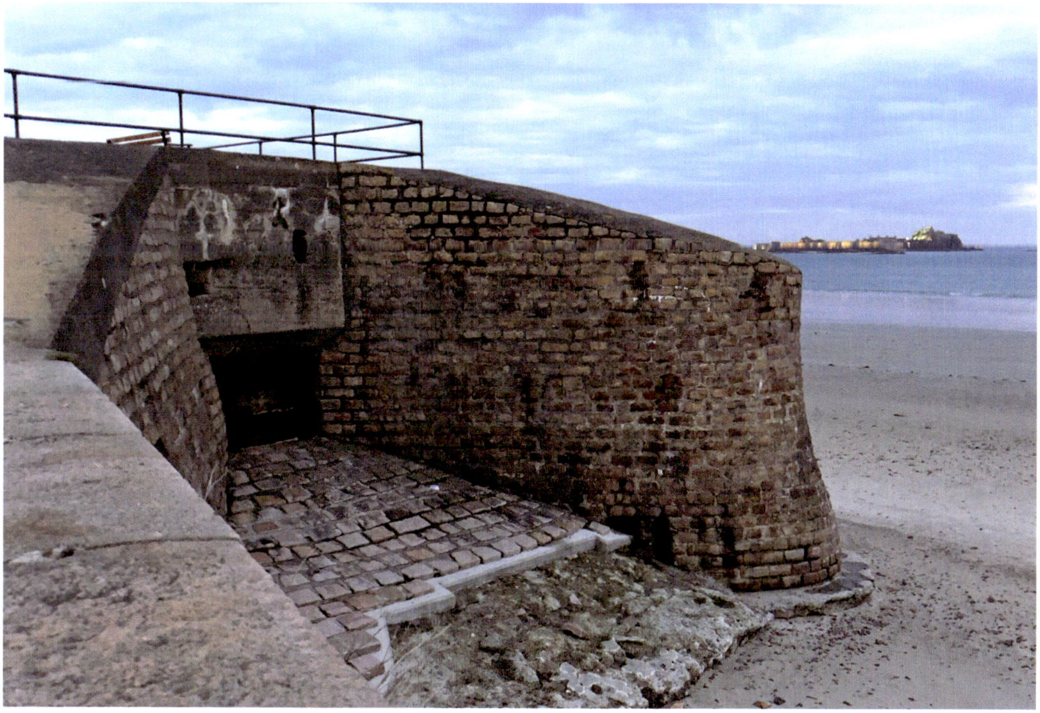

Resistance Nest First Tower, clad in Jersey granite. (Author's collection)

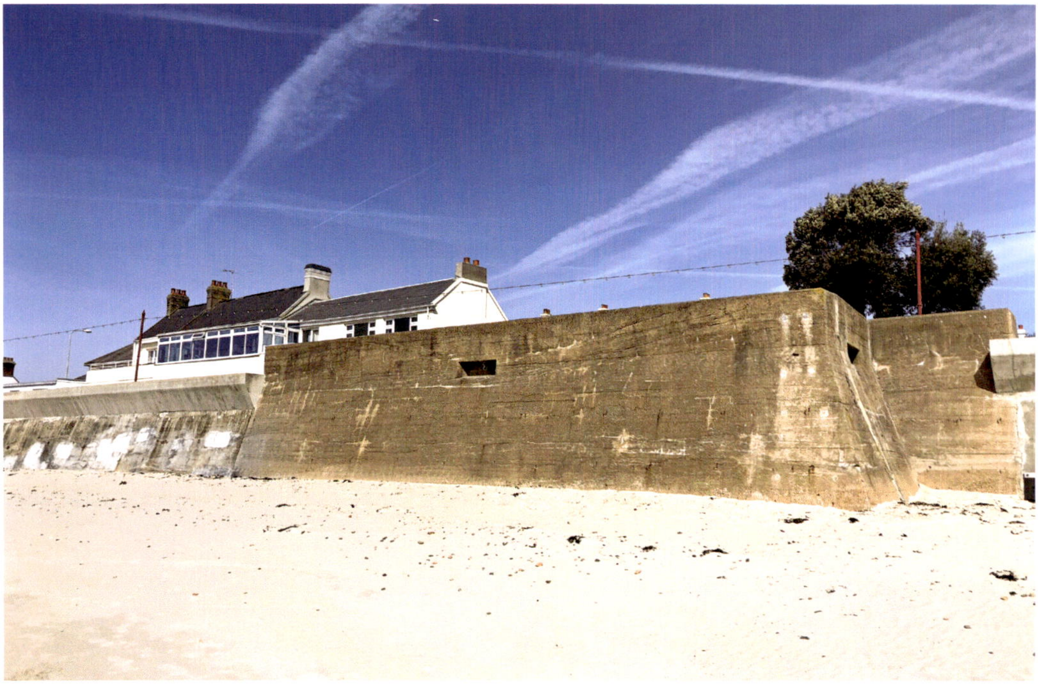

A 'dummy' bunker built into the anti-tank wall. (Author's collection)

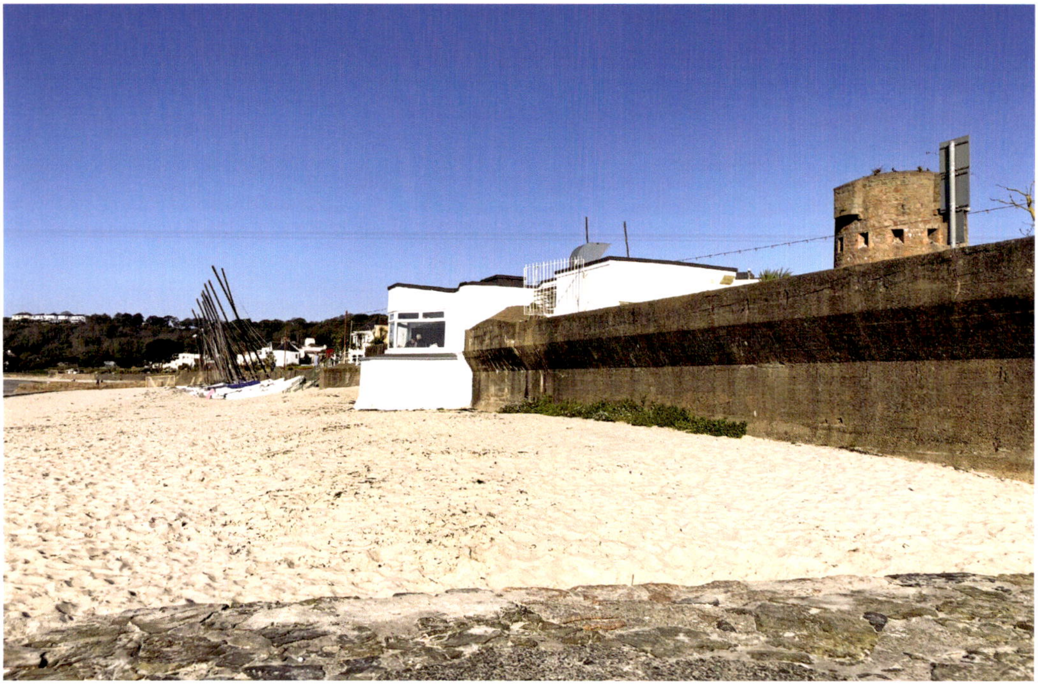

The German 'Resistance Nest Third Tower' has since been turned into the 'Gunsite Café'. (Author's collection)

St Ouen's Bay

Spanning almost the entire length of the west coast of Jersey, St Ouen's Bay has miles of flat golden sand and the rolling waves of the Atlantic Ocean crashing into it each day. During the German occupation of Jersey in the Second World War, such a vast open expanse of land would have been an obvious landing ground for any potential Allied liberation of the island, and the occupying forces wasted no time in building a number of defences right along this beautiful stretch of Jersey.

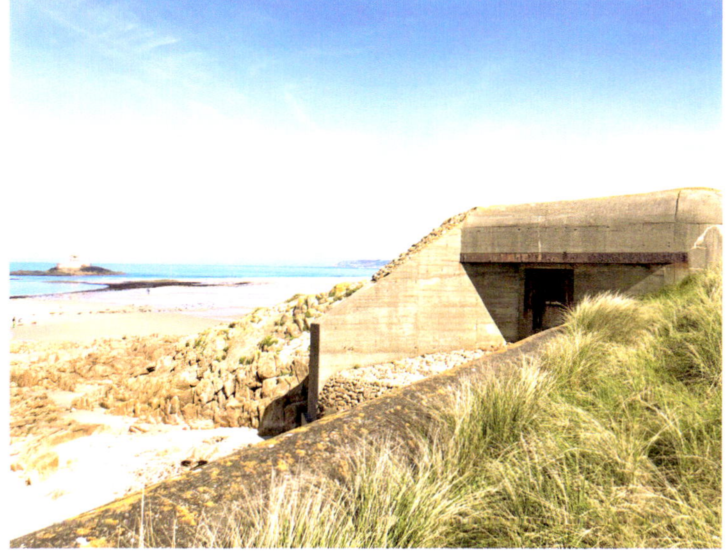

A German bunker overlooking St Ouen's Bay. (Author's collection)

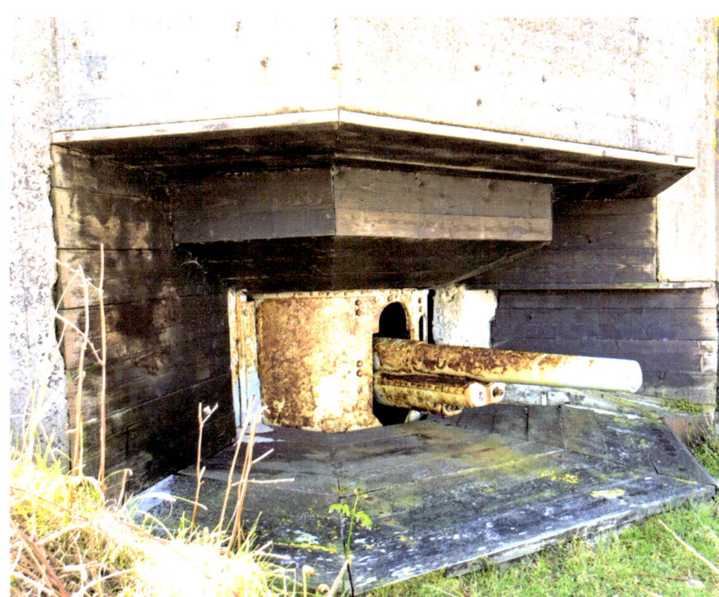

The rusting gun from the German occupation. (Author's collection)

Saint Peter's Barracks

St Peter's Barracks was one of the largest military establishments in Jersey and was responsible for the training of countless troops on the island. In 1939, the barracks housed the Royal Army Service Corps' Workshops and Technical School, although the training here obviously stopped when the islands were demilitarised. After the war, the army no longer needed the site and it was sold in 1948. The barracks were demolished to make way for further airport expansion.

Strongpoint Corbière

Corbière was an obvious location for German troops to build defensive positions during the occupation in the Second World War. At the southern end of the vast stretch of sand at St Ouen's Bay, and the point closest to any potential Allied shipping heading into the bay of St Malo, construction of the strongpoint took place between 1942 and 1943. It was made to 'Fortress' standard, which saw the external walls of the six fortifications built here having a thickness of an impressive 2 metres. The 2nd Company of Machine Gun Battalion 16 were stationed here, which meant a garrison of around 800–900 men saw out the duration of the war with the iconic Corbière lighthouse always in their vision. The lighthouse was manned by the German Navy, who operated the light and a radio post from there.

At the lower end of the headland, nearest to the lighthouse, is a bunker for a 60 cm searchlight. It could find targets up to 3.5 km away and was wheeled in and out of the bunker as required. Next to it is a casemate known as K1, which had a French gun installed. The German Army had acquired a number of these from the surrender of the French in 1940 and used them in bunkers – taking them off their original wheeled carriages and mounting them onto a fixed position.

Another 10.5 cm coastal defensive casemate, known as K2, was built into the hillside to cover the approaches to Petit Port Bay and St Ouen's Bay and is one of the bunkers that have been restored and maintained by CIOS. There are a number of other personnel shelters, machine-gun emplacements and small rifle nests across the headland and a remarkable set of bunkers in the middle of the site.

Restored by the CIOS to its original wartime appearance, there is a Type 634 – a six-loopholed machine-gun turret bunker that was a focal point of Strongpoint Corbière. On slightly higher ground than its neighbour, there were six armoured periscopes, along with radio communications that meant observations and commands for the whole site would have been sent from here. Close by is a Type 633 M19 mortar bunker than has a staggering 40-ton steel turret! From here, 5 cm mortar bombs could be fired at a range of 875 metres. What makes these two bunkers so impressive is the long underground passage that links them, and walking through this tunnel, followed by climbing up a ladder to get into the mortar bunker, is an experience the German troops during the Second World War would have done countless times.

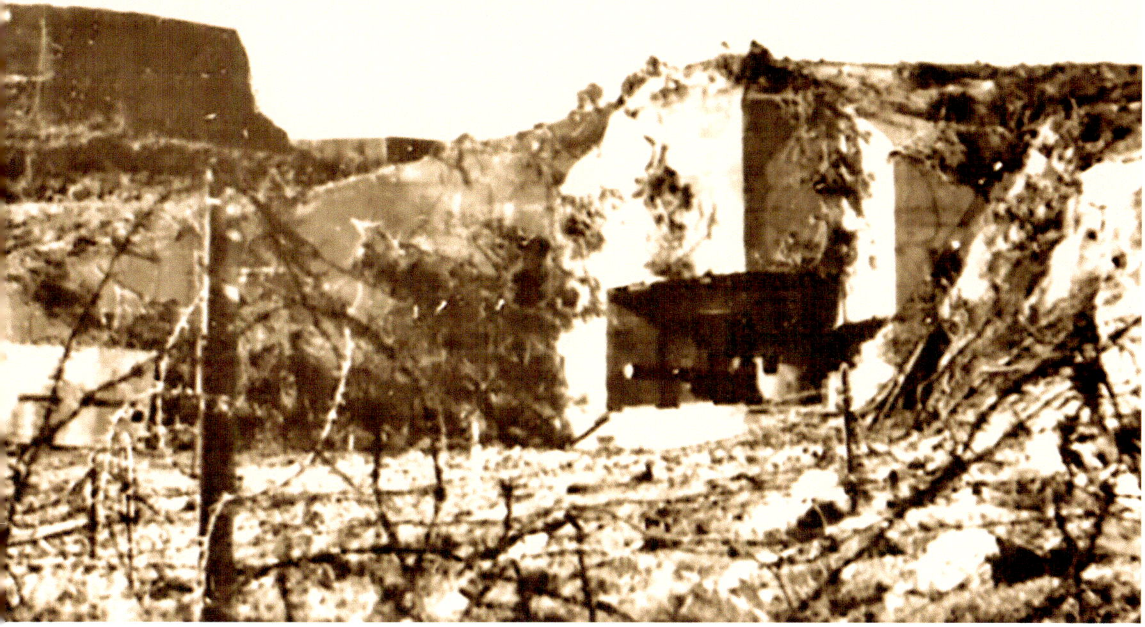

Strongpoint Corbière during the occupation. (Courtesy of the Channel Island Occupation Society (Jersey))

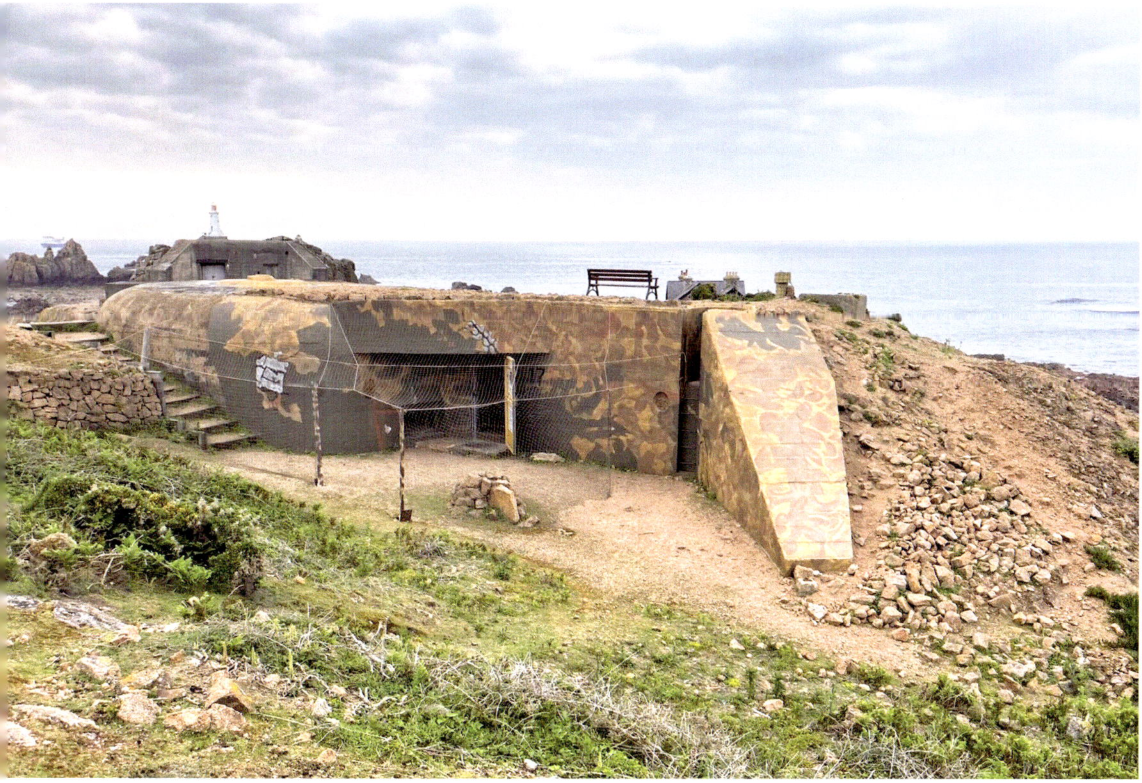

Strongpoint Corbière today. (Courtesy of the Channel Island Occupation Society (Jersey))

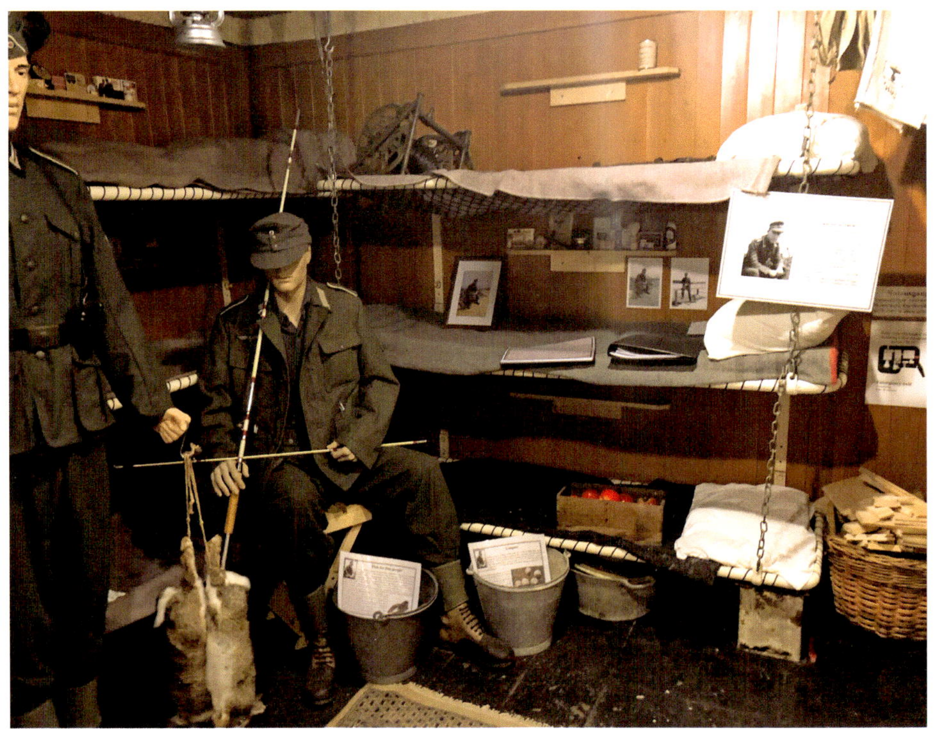

One of the many rooms that have been restored to how it would have looked during the occupation. (Author's collection)

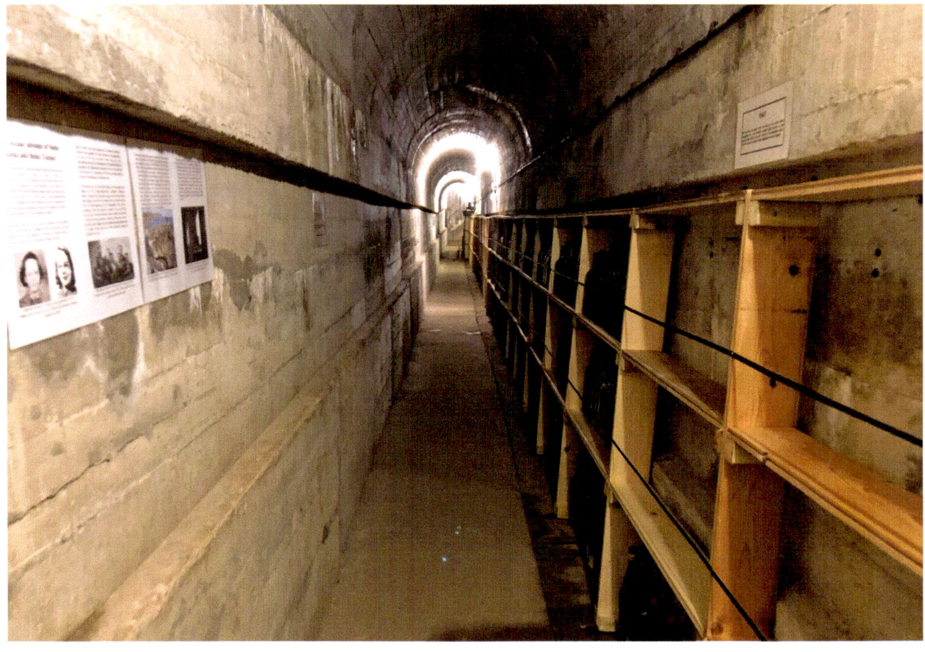

The long underground connecting corridor between two bunkers. (Author's collection)

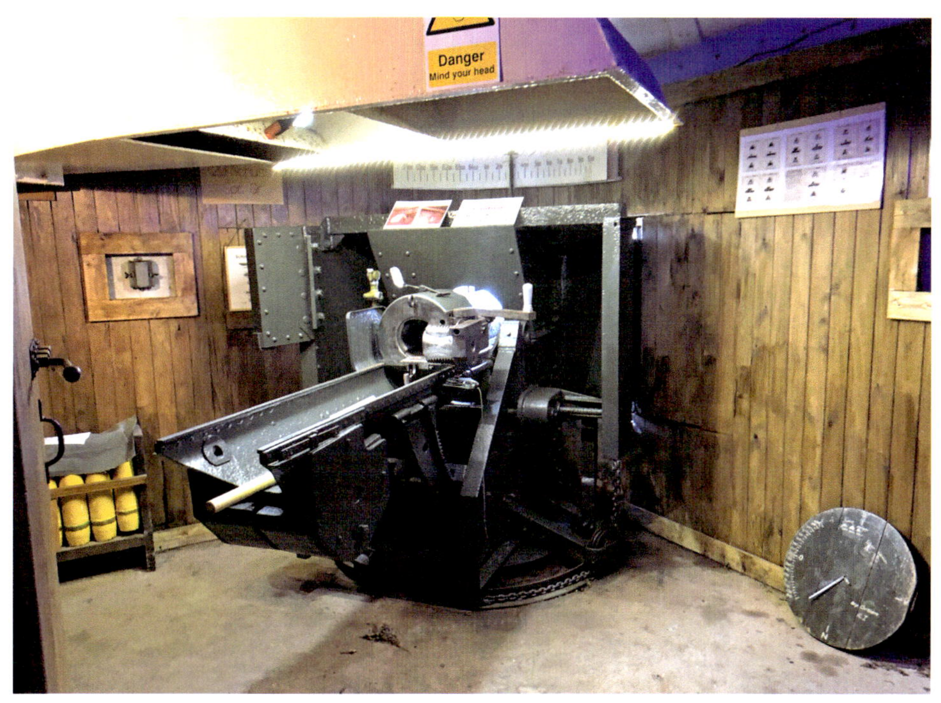

The original 10.5 cm gun still inside the K2 casemate bunker. (Author's collection)

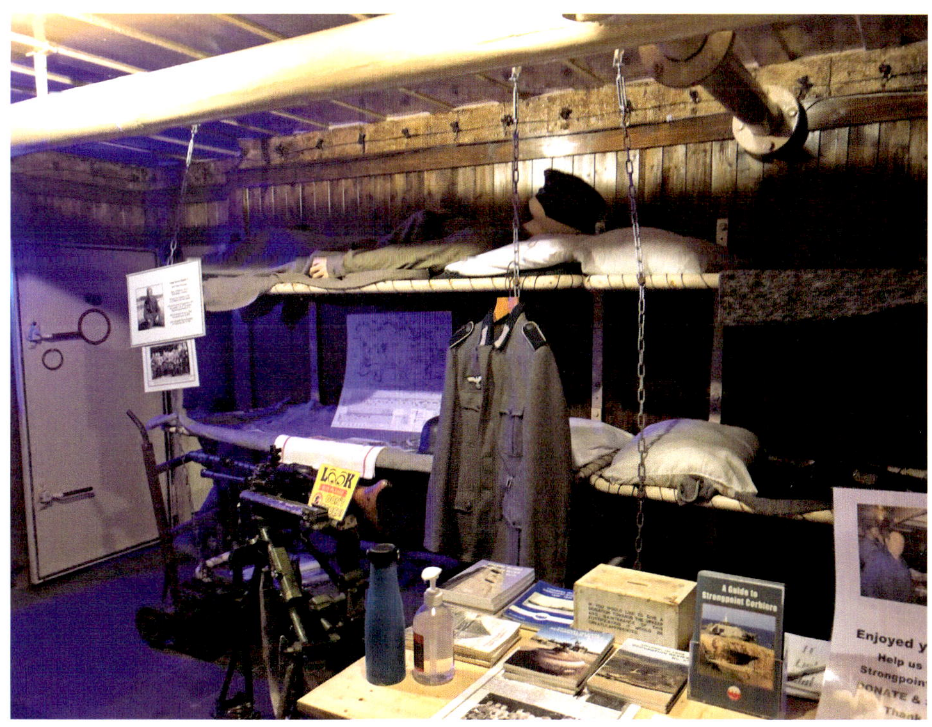

The living quarters inside the K2 casemate. (Author's collection)

CHAPTER 2

Guernsey

Castle Cornet

As the vast majority of people visiting Guernsey do so by sea, they will more than likely head into St Peter Port, and pass by the rather impressive Castle Cornet. The original keep, curtain walls and courtyards were built by 1250 on a tidal island that is around 600 metres off the mainland and covers nearly 5 acres. Sitting as it does at the entrance to the harbour, it has seen a fair bit of military action over the last 800 years. In 1339 a French force captured the castle, and the island of Guernsey, and made improvements to the defences, before it was taken back in 1345. Thirteen years later, in 1358, the French returned and again captured the castle but this time their occupation only lasted a year.

It wasn't all defeat and capture though. In 1372 Owain Lawgoch, a claimant to the Welsh throne, attacked Guernsey and besieged Castle Cornet, but was unable to take it. The early fifteenth century saw more improvements made, with the addition of new towers, and a French assault in 1461 was unsuccessful. As with all castles, the development of the cannon and the use of gunpowder saw significant redesigning taking place, including the curtain wall being strengthened in 1570, with the Royal Battery being completed in 1594.

The English Civil Wars of 1642–1651 saw the castle supporting the Royalist cause whilst the Island of Guernsey itself supported the Parliamentarian cause. In 1642, the castle cannons fired onto St Peter Port. Castle Cornet held out for nine long years thanks to support from Royalist supporting Jersey, until the castle surrendered on 17 December 1651, with the garrison being allowed to march out and leave the Island.

The castle served as official residence of the governor of Guernsey until 30 December 1672 – when lightning struck the magazine of the castle, destroying the keep and a number of other buildings! The governor's residence moved to the island and the castle was used partly as a prison. The Napoleonic Wars saw an additional barracks added to the site, and after these wars, a breakwater joined the castle to the mainland. During the Second World War, a small detachment of German troops were garrisoned at the castle and built some concrete casemates and machine-gun nests, particularly on the Citadel. In 1947, the Crown presented the castle to the people of Guernsey as a token of their loyalty during the two world wars.

Today, it is possible to explore Castle Cornet by entering the castle from its Main Gate and then navigating through the Outer Ward and Barbican before finally reaching the Citadel at the top.

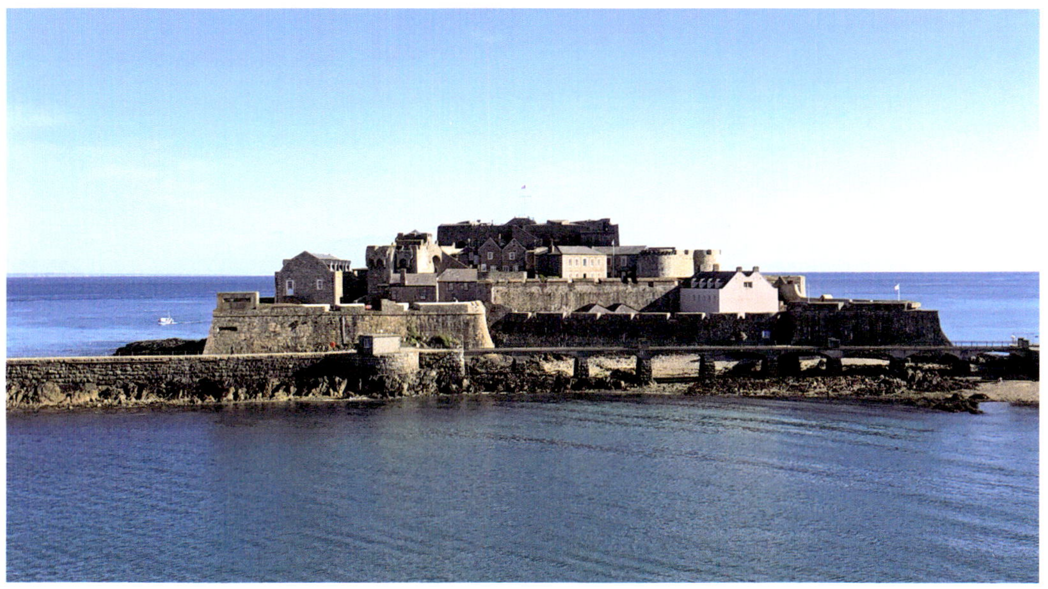

A view of Castle Cornet from the sea. (Author's collection)

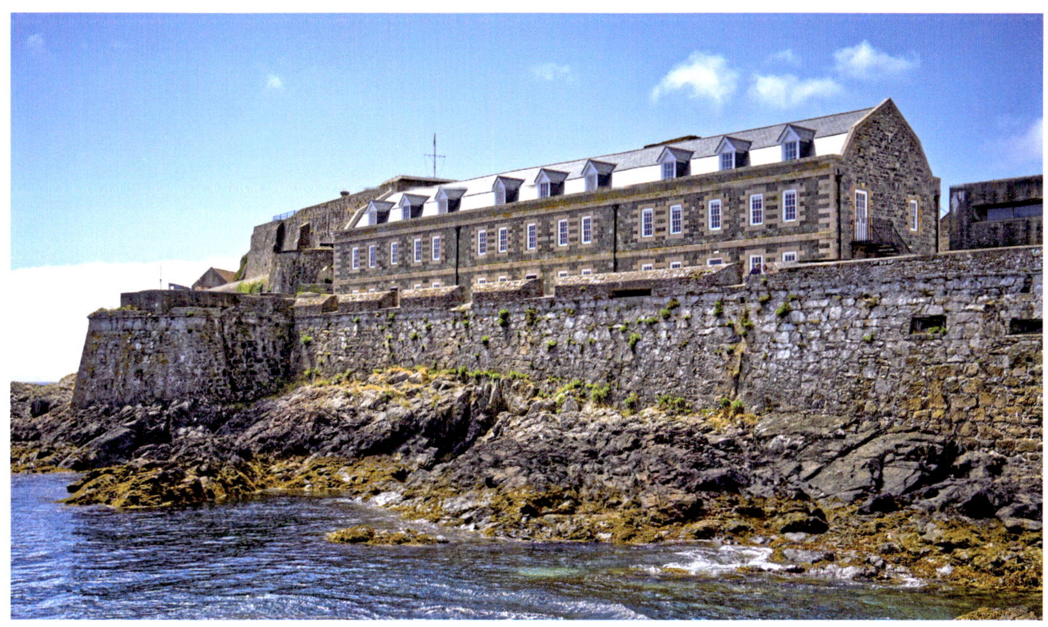

Looking back towards the castle from the harbour lighthouse. (Courtesy of Geoff Hansen CC BY-ND 2.0)

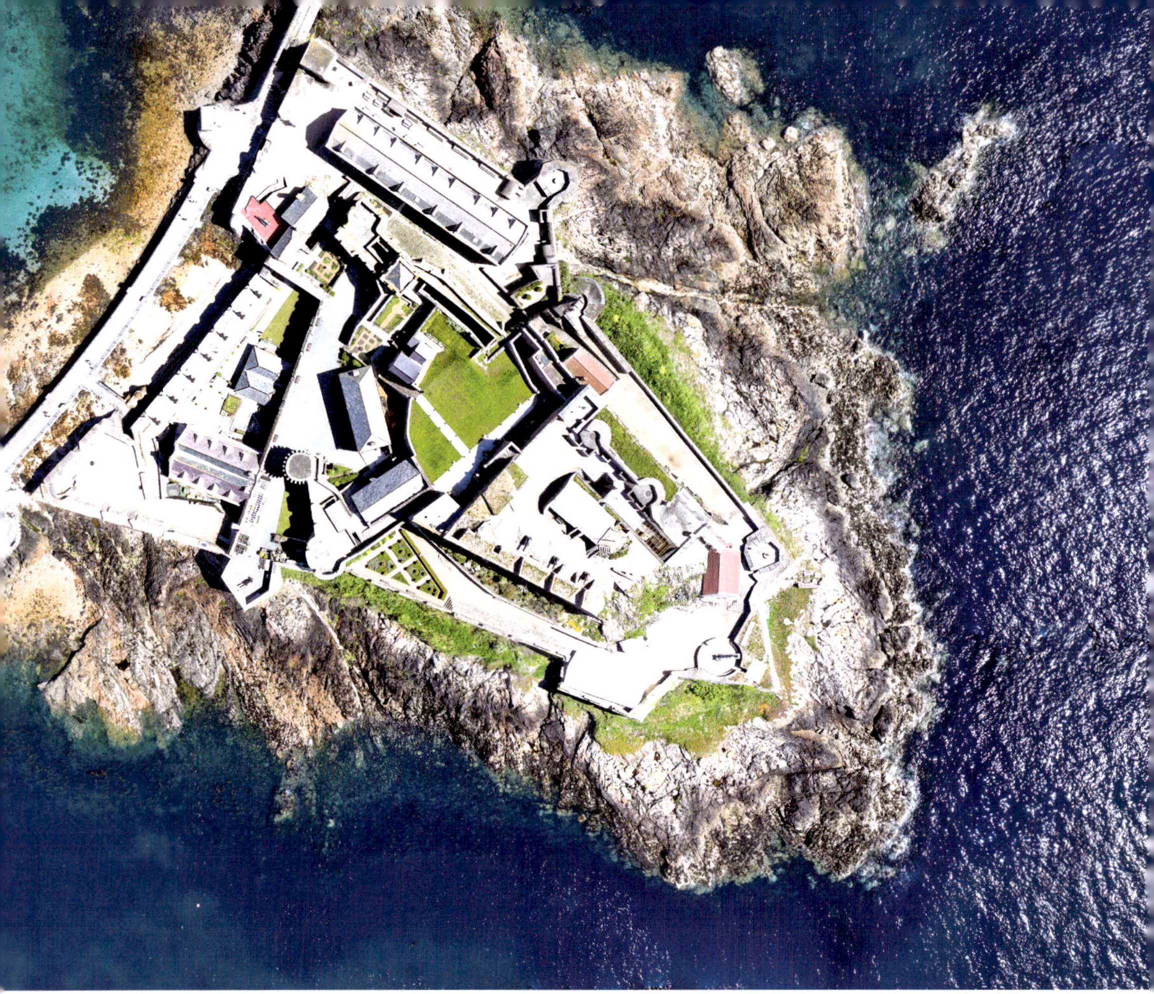

A spectacular shot of Castle Cornet from above. (Public domain)

Chateau des Marais

Chateau des Marais is a typical motte-and-bailey castle that was first built in 1170, with a ditch, surrounding wall and raised mound. Located on a small rocky hill in the north of the island, it was in an area of marshland that would have offered it some protection from invaders – particularly pirates. The importance of Chateau des Marais didn't last long, however, as the construction of Castle Cornet in 1250 shifted the focal point of the island's defences to St Peter Port, and the Chateau des Marais gradually became a ruin. Locally known as 'Ivy Castle', towards the end of the eighteenth century, the castle was refortified because of the threat posed by French forces. The ditch was renewed, stone walls were built up around the chateau, and musket firing steps were built. Inside, a barracks, magazine and other associated buildings were constructed. Although it was garrisoned by a small force, it never really saw any action, and after the Napoleonic Wars ended it became the Governor's garden! During the Second World War, German troops built a bunker, machine gun posts and trenches.

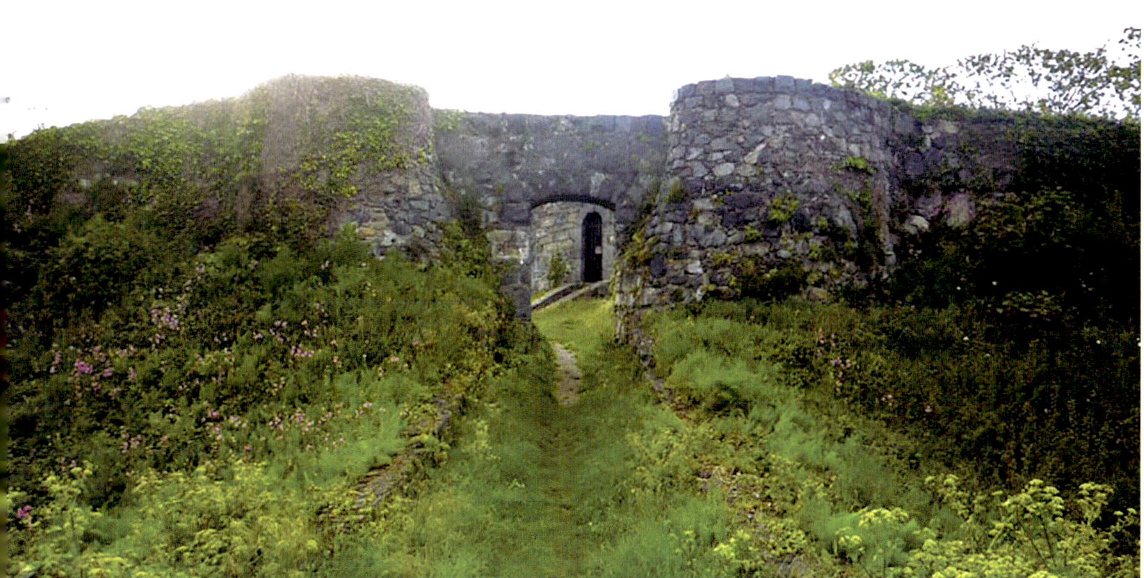

The entrance up to the small Chateau des Marais. (Public domain)

Fort Doyle

Fort Doyle was built in 1805 at Fontenelle Bay on the northern side of Guernsey – being one of the many defences constructed in the early part of the nineteenth century as a result of a possible French invasion. Originally armed with three 18-pounder cannons, in the 1860s these were replaced with two traversing cannons, which would have made it easier to cover the approach to the bay. By the beginning of the twentieth century, the fort was used as a lighthouse to guide shipping, but during the Second World War, German forces fortified the north of the island, with Fort Doyle having an anti-aircraft gun installed

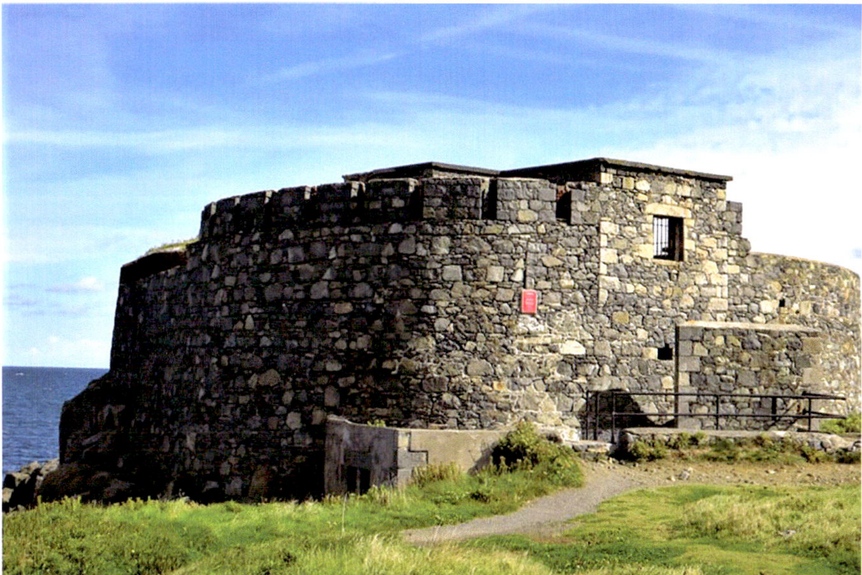

Fort Doyle, on the north of the island. (Courtesy of Ben Smitheon CC BY-SA 2.0)

Fort George

The Anglo-French War of 1778–1783 saw planning begin for a new fort in Guernsey that would be capable of accommodating the larger number of troops that were now stationed on the island – one and a half regiments had moved into the island following the start of the American War of Independence a few years earlier. The locals in Guernsey were required to billet any soldiers that could not be accommodated in the current military headquarters at Castle Cornet, and this understandably had begun to cause problems with such large numbers.

Construction started in 1780 and Fort George was to become the main military headquarters on the island – located in St Peter Port and close to the established Castle Cornet. Fully completed in 1812, the main entrance to the fort is through a large gateway that, to this day, still has the original wooden gates. Immediately behind this, a moat and a drawbridge provided a second line of defence from a landward attack, and inside a large barracks area would have been able to accommodate approximately 3,000 soldiers. Numerous associated buildings were built, including an armoury, infantry hospital and water storage tank, as well as a number of tunnels under the fort. The parade ground was opposite the impressive 7,000 square foot Governor's house, Belvedere House, which lay at the edge of the fort.

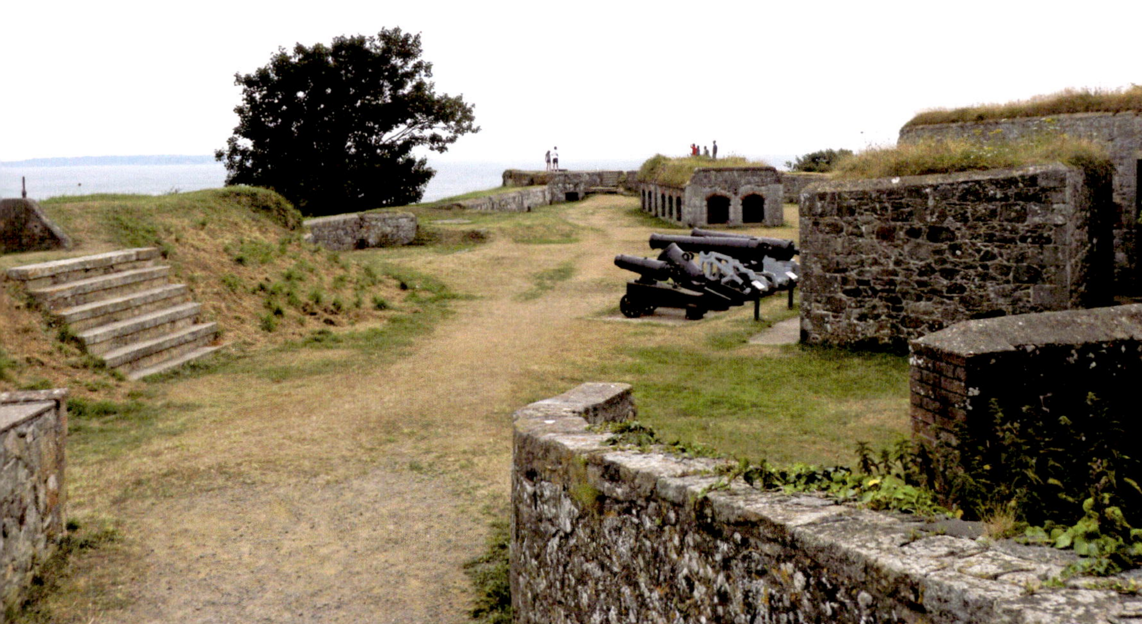

Today not much remains of Fort George. (Courtesy of Manxruler CC BY-SA 2.0)

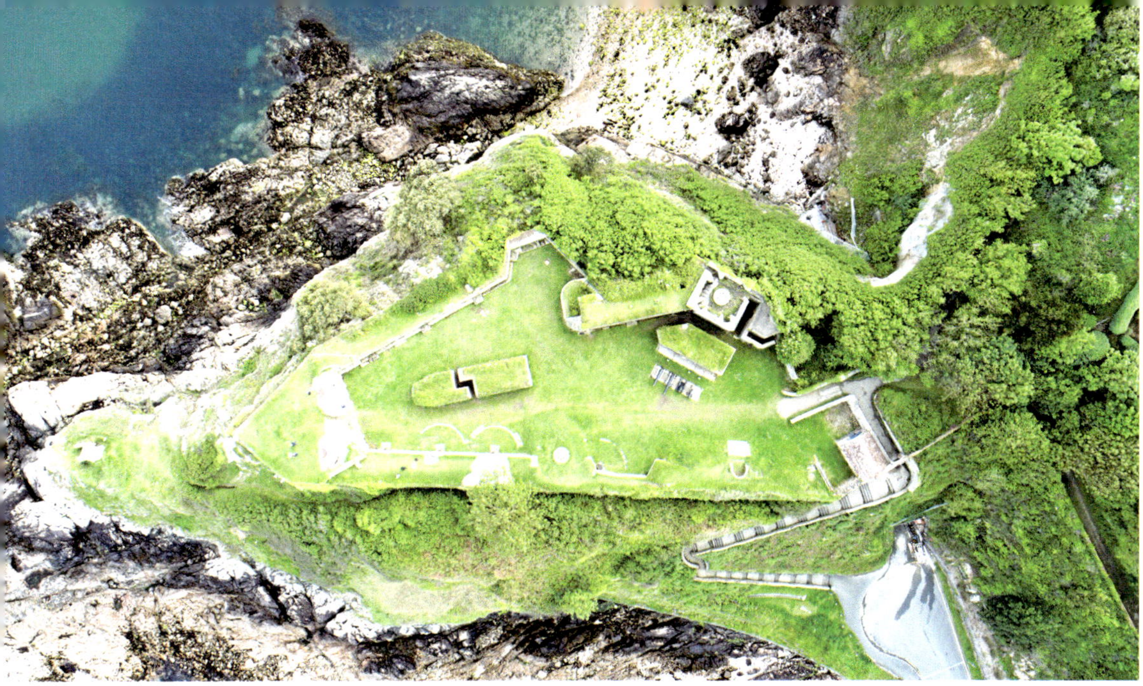

An aerial view of Clarence Battery. (Public domain)

By 1833, the official list of defences at the fort was thirty-four mounted cannons, one carronade and four mortars. On the seaward side of the fort was a battery that had ten gun mounts that could fire in two directions from the small headland it was on, along with a guard house and magazine. Originally called 'Terres Point Battery' when it was built in 1780, it was renamed 'Clarence Battery' in 1815 and the original guns were later replaced with two 5-inch guns at the very tip of the battery.

During the Second World War, German troops understandably utilised the location, installing a 3.7 cm flak battery, numerous machine-gun nests and a searchlight. In June 1944, the Allied forces bombed the fort in order to destroy the radar station there ahead of the D-Day landings in nearby Normandy, and after the war, it lay derelict for a number of years. A military cemetery has been on site for centuries, with graves of British soldiers and sailors from the nineteenth and twentieth centuries, and over 100 German graves from the Second World War. Today, only the Main Gate and Clarence Battery remain, with the rest of the site having been sold off for the development of private luxury housing.

Fort Grey

Built on a tidal rock in Rocquaine Bay on the west coast of Guernsey, Fort Grey was constructed on the site of a late medieval small fort or chateau. Named after Charles Grey, 1st Earl Grey, who was Governor of Guernsey from 1797 to 1807, this Martello tower was one of three constructed in 1804 during the Napoleonic War. Each of these towers had a 24-pounder carronade on the roof to protect the tower, which also acted as the 'Keep' to its surrounding battery, and as well as defending the location, it was also designated a warning

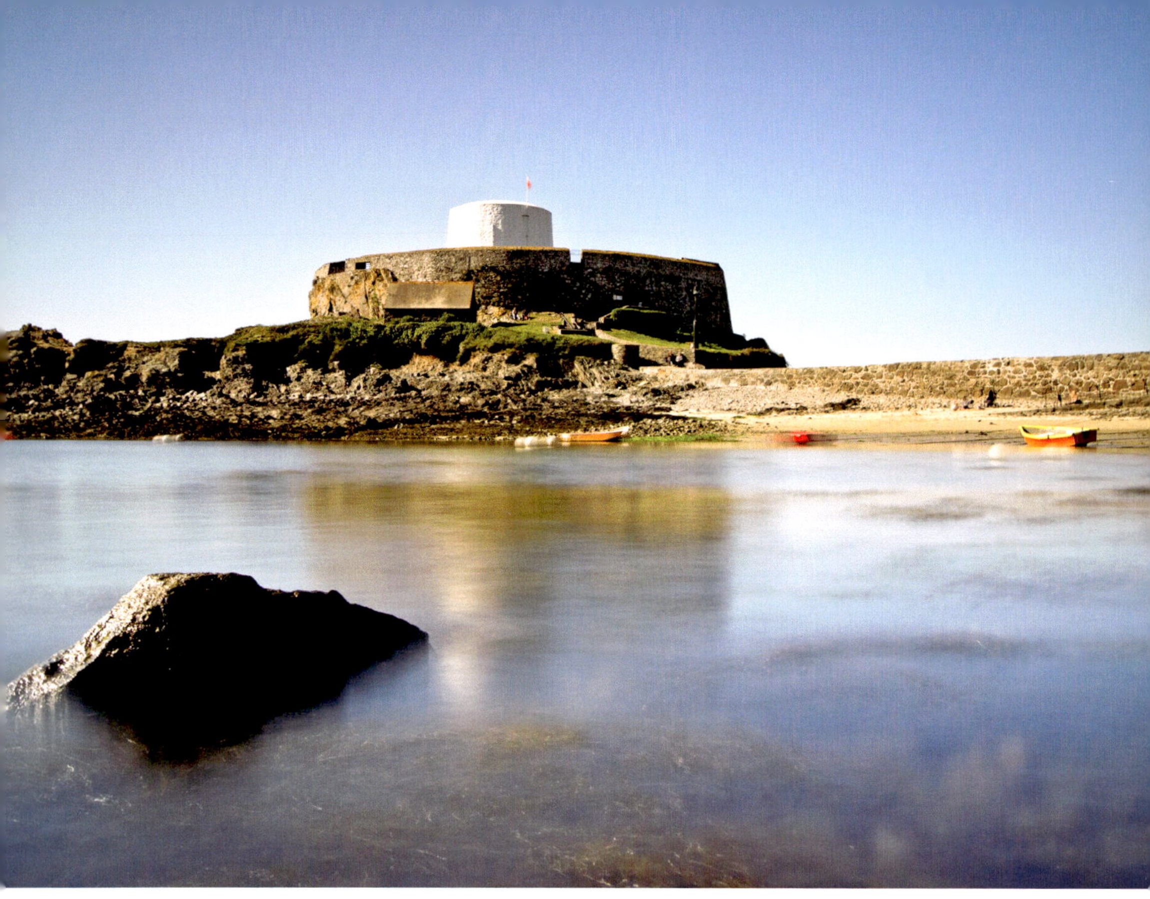

Fort Grey, also known locally as the 'cup and saucer'. (Courtesy of Angus MacRae CC BY 2.0)

gun that would be fired if a French invasion happened. In 1891, the States of Guernsey purchased the tower from the Crown. In the Second World War, German forces installed a 3.7 cm Pak 36 anti-tank gun, and machine guns, as the fort became a 'resistance nest'. Today, it acts as a shipwreck museum and nearby there is a monument to MV *Prosperity*, who was lost in nearby waters on the night of 16/17 January 1974.

Fort Hommet

Fort Hommet sits on the Vazon Bay headland, with the first gun being placed here in 1680. It would seem that the attempted French invasion of Jersey in 1781 made Guernsey improve its own defences, with more gun positions added in 1795. By 1805, six guns were here and the road connecting the fort and St Peter Port was upgraded, but most importantly was the building of a Martello tower. One of only three on the island, a 24-pounder carronade was mounted on the roof and the tower at Fort Hommet also had an exterior staircase to the second floor. The Victorian era saw new batteries and barracks added to the site, with the redevelopment being completed by 1852 when 68-pounder and 8-inch shell guns replaced some of the 24-pounder guns that were installed in the batteries.

When Germany occupied Guernsey during the Second World War, they designated the whole of the Vazon Bay headland a strongpoint, adding numerous new fortifications to the area, and, of course, Fort Hammet. The Martello tower had two bunkers dug into it for holding a 60 cm and a huge 150 cm searchlight, with the crews living in the tower too. Two casemates with large 10.5 cm guns were dug into the north facing ground, another two facing south across Vazon beach and an additional bunker looking west. At the centre of the headland, a mortar bunker was built, along with personnel shelters and an anti-tank gun emplacement. Add to this barbed wire, flamethrowers, machine-gun nests and some large minefields (according to records, minefield 27 had 417 S-mines, 464 Teller mines and 624 captured British mines), this was a well-defended headland.

After Guernsey was liberated, the vast majority of the metal was removed for scrap, before most of the German built bunkers were buried in an effort to return the landscape to its pre-war condition. However, one of the bunkers has been restored as a museum and it is possible to visit.

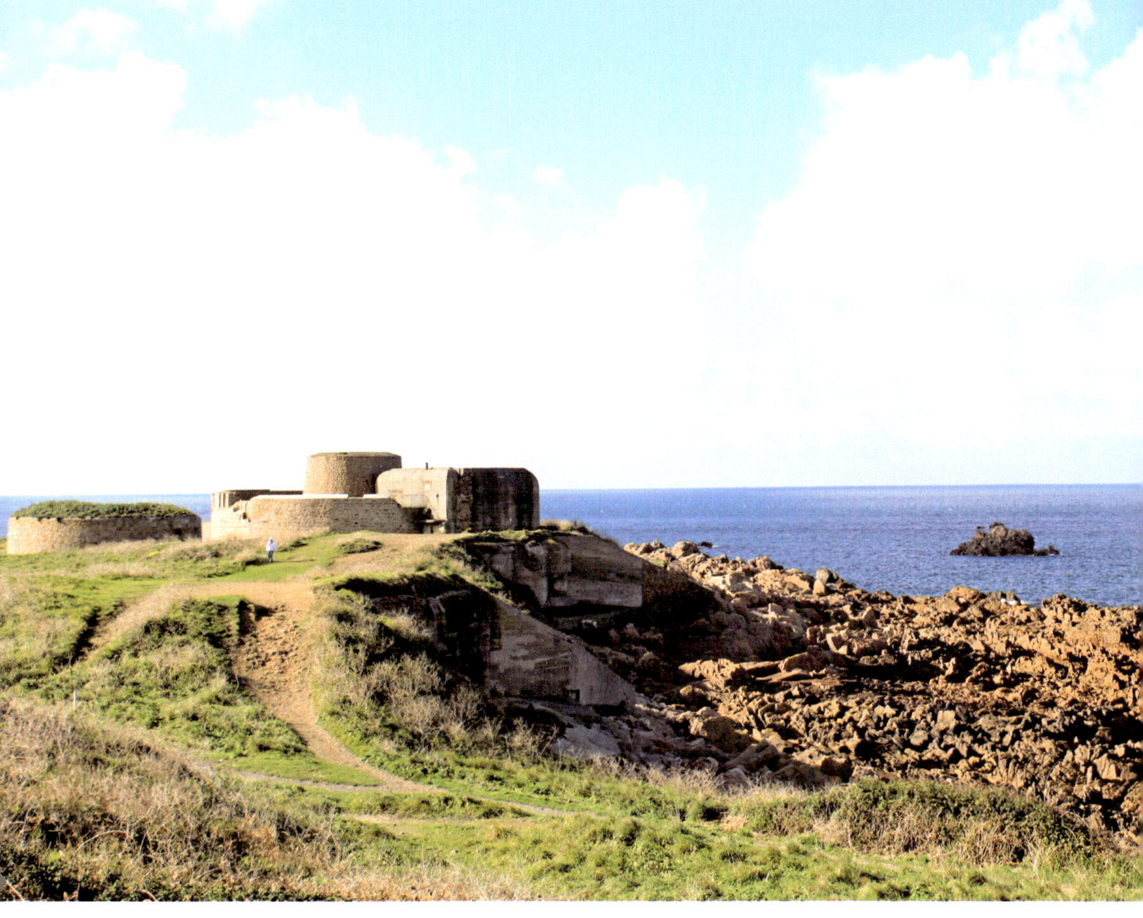

Fort Hommet. (Courtesy of Dave Paterson CC BY 2.0)

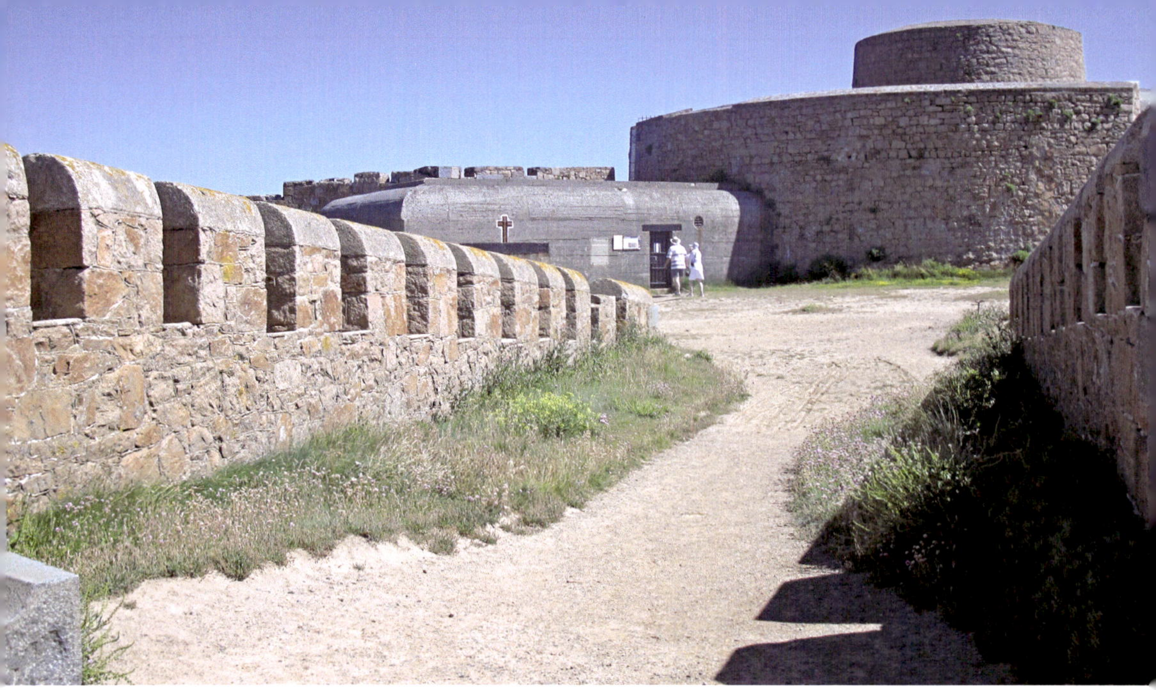

A mixture of Victorian era crenelations and Second World War German positions. (Public domain)

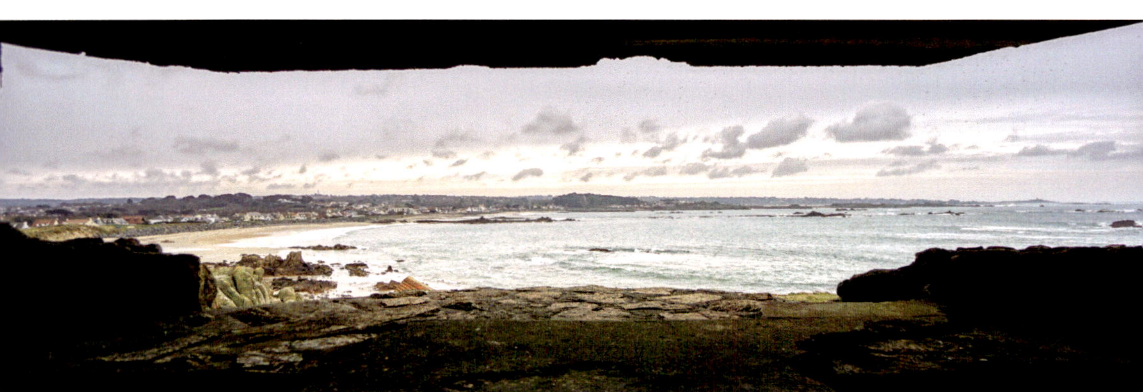

A view from a gun emplacement at Fort Hommet on Vazon Bay headland. (Courtesy of Simon Morris CC BY-ND 2.0)

Fort Pembroke

Built in 1811 on the headland overlooking L'Ancresse Bay, Fort Pembroke was designed to offer protection to the northern coast of the island. When completed, it had mounted guns, and the plan was for the fort to work in tandem with the single gun Platon Battery situated around 100 metres away. After the threat of French invasion had passed, the Crown sold the site in 1922 to a local quarrying company, and in the Second World War, although the German troops didn't man the fort, they did place minefields and an anti-tank wall along the beach.

Fort Richmond

Overlooking Perelle Bay, Fort Richmond is another coastal defence position built to help defend the island from French invasion. Built in 1855, the outline of the building is much as it was when it was built and given that there was accommodation, artillery casements and a range of associated buildings, it is no surprise that it was used by German occupying forces in the Second World War. Recently, it was sold for development as a private residence.

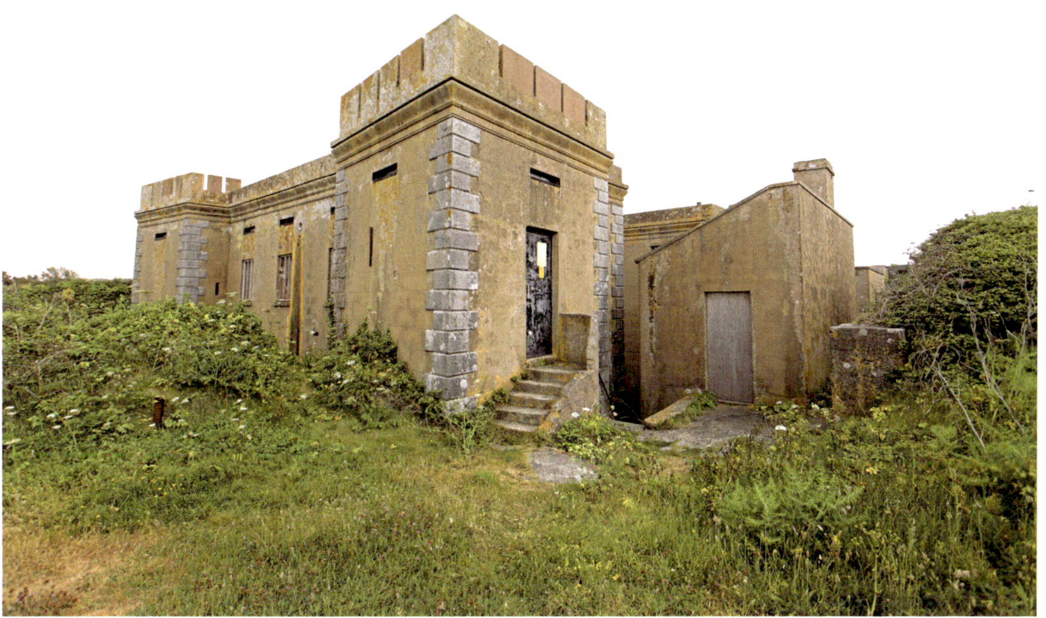

The ruined state of Fort Richmond. (Courtesy of Th. Philipp CC BY-SA 4.0)

Fort Saumarez

Located on the headland on the northern tip of L'Erée, Fort Saumarez was a defensive Martello tower that was constructed in 1804 on the footprint of an earlier battery. It had a 24-pounder carronade on the roof to protect the battery and the surrounding area, and because of its excellent range of vision, it also served as an optical telegraph station that would give warning of any approaching vessels. As with the other Martello towers on the island, Fort Saumarez received an armament upgrade in 1852, with 32-pounder guns and 8-inch shell guns replacing some of the 24-pounder guns mounted here. During the Second World War, the German forces recognised the usefulness of the location and built a four-storey concrete observation tower on top of the existing tower. In the years after the war, the surrounding battery was demolished, and the site is now privately owned.

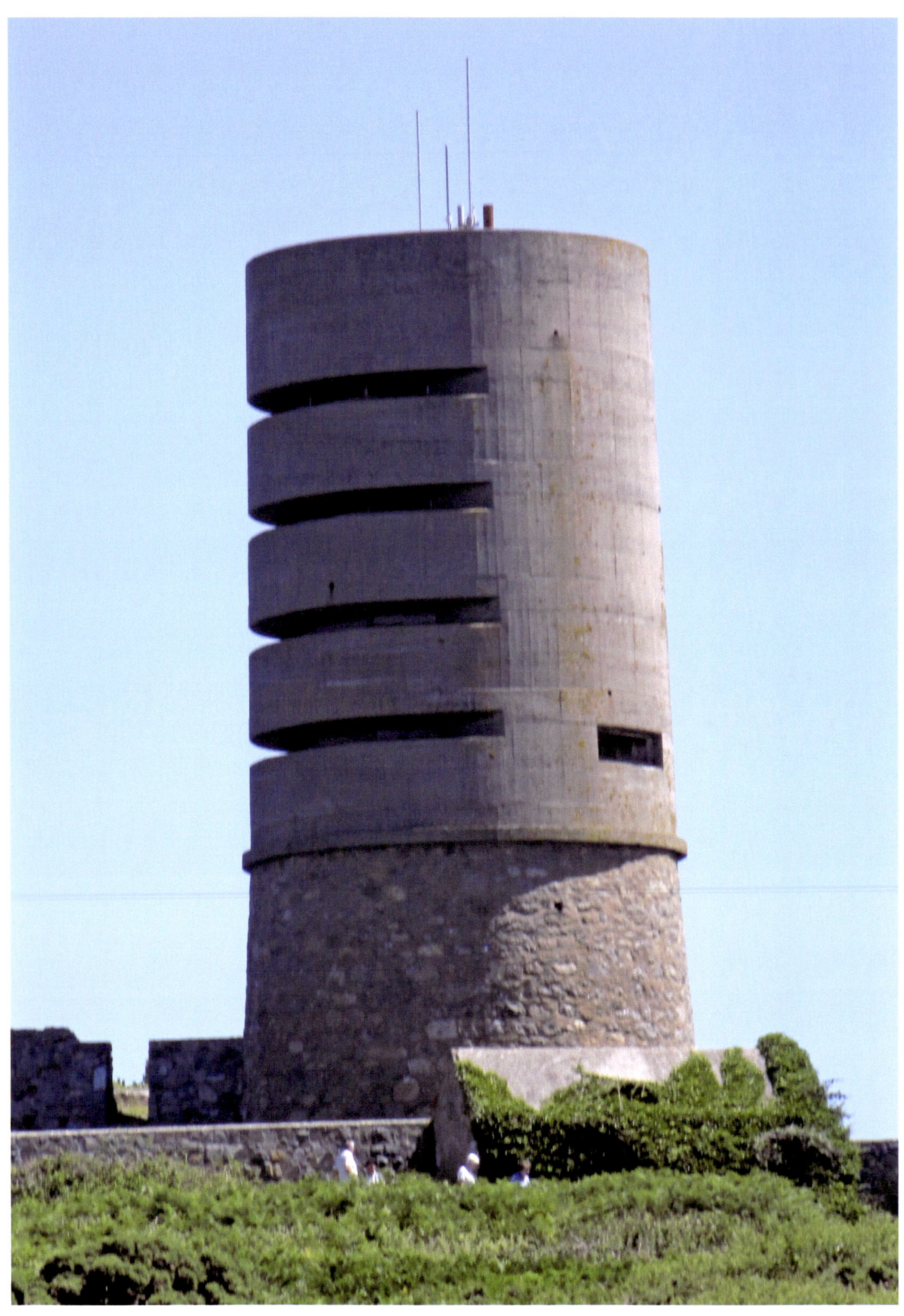

The German Observation Tower added to Fort Saumarez's Martello tower. (Public domain)

Grandes Rocques Fort

Located at the far side of Grandes Rocques beach, the fort was likely constructed towards the end of the eighteenth century and would have had 24-pounder guns, to help protect the island. German occupying forces made modifications to the fort during the Second World War with bunkers, machine-gun nests and observation points being added. Today it is open all year round having been left to the elements since the 1940s.

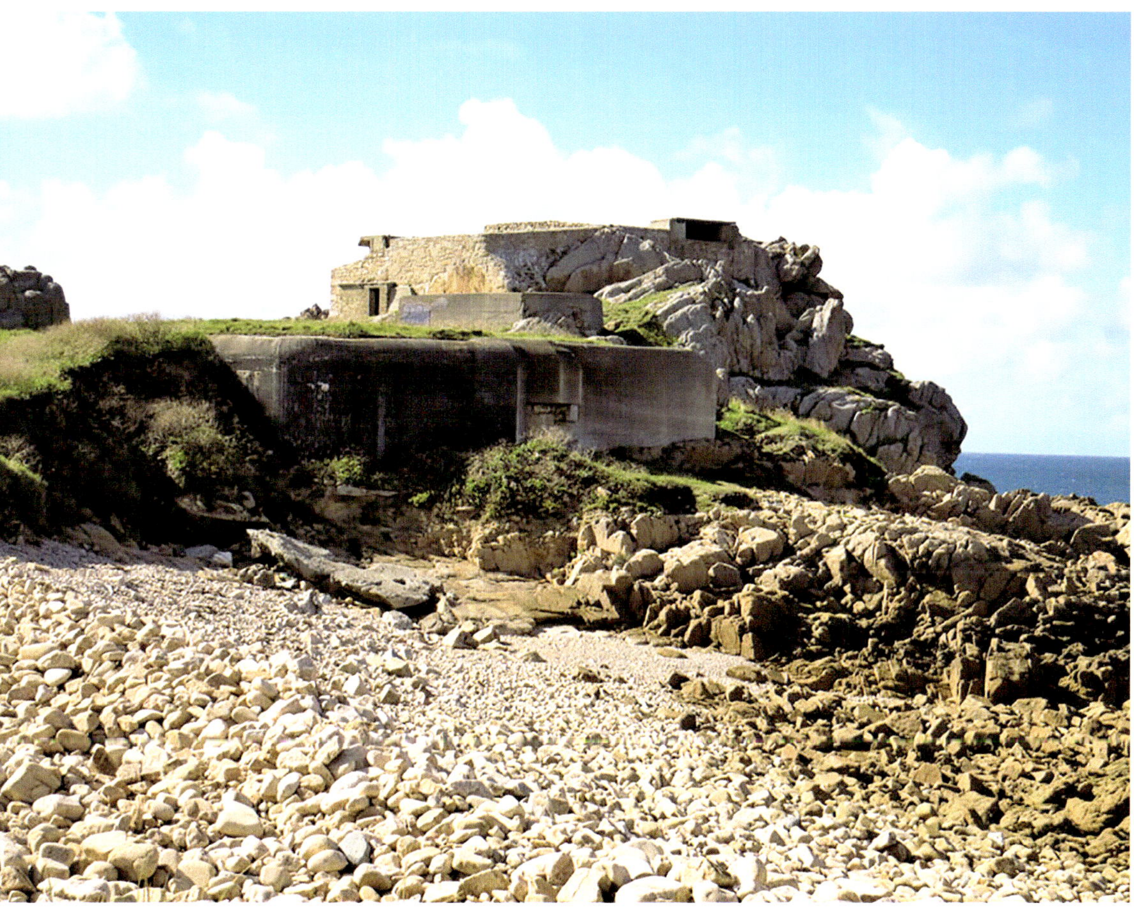

Grandes Rocques Fort, with a more recent bunker from the Second World War in front. (Courtesy of Ben Smitheon CC BY-SA 2.0)

Guernsey Militia

Like their neighbours in Jersey, the island of Guernsey had a local band of militia who had promised to defend the island from foreign invaders, and the very first beginnings of this stretches all the way back to 1203. The earliest recorded 'skirmish' took place in 1214, when

Eustace the Monk, a pirate based in Sark, attacked the island, only to be met by this newly raised and locally armed force comprising the whole manhood of the island! At the end of the century the island was invaded, and Castle Cornet held for a number of years, before another French invasion attempt was made in 1336. Stopped by the men on the island, the militia was officially recognised in 1337.

In 1338, the Guernsey Militia had its first official battle, beating a French invasion force that had landed at Les Hubits. However, they returned a year later and took the island, holding the island for twelve months, and Castle Cornet for five years! A further French incursion happened in 1358, with the militia eventually claiming it back a year later. In 1372 Owain Lawgoch, a claimant to the Welsh throne, attacked Guernsey and killed 400 of the island militia, before retreating.

Weekly training began in each parish, using common land often near a church, and a French attack in 1461 was stopped in its tracks. As with the Jersey Militia, tactics and organisation evolved, and during the fifteenth and sixteenth centuries, each of the ten parishes took on more responsibility, raising a company of around 100 men commanded by a captain. Daily duties included attending reviews, practice and standing watch and by 1680, the militia was nearly 2,000 strong.

During the Third English Civil War, Guernsey and its militia supported the Parliamentarians, whilst Castle Cornet was Royalist, but it took a staggering eight years for the garrison to surrender!

Between August 1778 and March 1779, fifteen Guernsey loophole towers were built across the coast of the island in an effort to deter possible French attacks. Standing at 9 metres tall, they were manned by the militia and provided a defensive position to fire muskets from.

On 27 March 1783 there was a mutiny in Guernsey by 500 regular soldiers from the recently created 104th Regiment, at Fort George. The 18th Regiment and Guernsey Militia responded, outflanking the rebel soldiers in a brief standoff, and ultimately forcing them to surrender.

In 1804, defences were strengthened right across the island. Three larger Martello towers were constructed and over sixty smaller gun emplacements and ammunition magazines were built to defend possible landing points by an enemy – all of these manned by the militia artillery regiment. There was a further restructuring of some of the militia units in 1825, and in 1850, the Town Arsenal was built and became the headquarters of the militia – further arsenals were built in 1882.

At the outbreak of the First World War in 1914, the Royal Guernsey Militia comprised of two infantry regiments and an artillery regiment, but technically they could not fight as a unit outside the island except to help the king regain his throne. So, in 1916 the militia was disbanded, making way for the Guernsey Light Infantry to be raised and a battalion was sent off to fight. 327 men were killed, 255 were taken prisoner and 667 were wounded. In the Second World War, Guernsey was demilitarised and so was the militia, with equipment being shipped to England to stop it falling into enemy hands. Today there is a Royal Guernsey Militia Museum located at Castle Cornet.

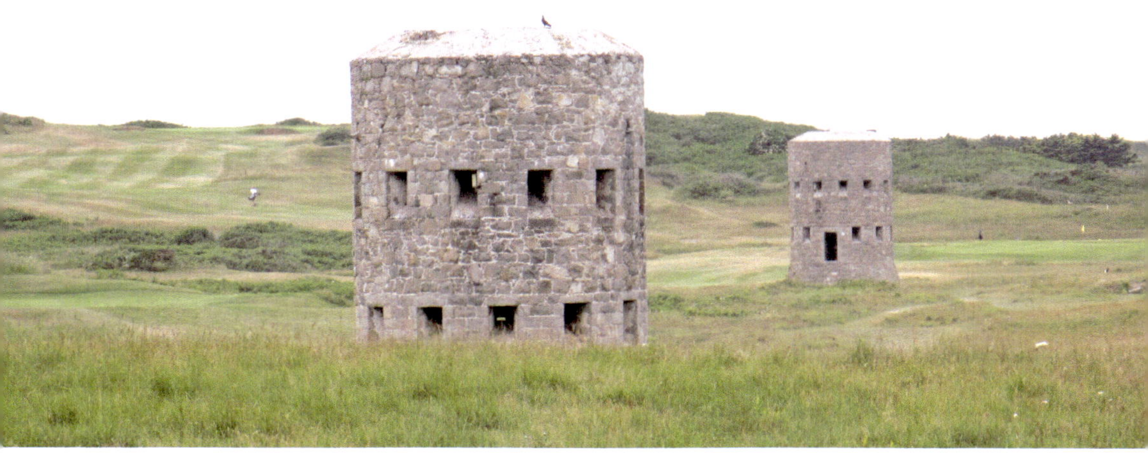

Two of the Guernsey loophole towers at L'Ancresse. (Public domain)

Havelet Half-moon Battery

Located in St Peter Port, Havelet half-moon battery covered Havelet Bay and was just one of the sixty smaller gun batteries constructed across the island in 1804. This position looked directly towards Castle Cornet, and today there is a restaurant in its location – the half-moon shape still clearly visible.

Mirus Battery

Built between November 1941 and June 1942 by the occupying German military, Mirus Battery is located in Saint Peter and Saint Saviour and is the largest battery in the Channel Islands. Spread over nearly a square kilometre, there were four 30.5 cm guns, capable of firing a shell every 60–90 seconds up to 50 km in distance.

Each of these gun emplacements had a 21-metre circular concrete pit, which allowed the armoured turret to rotate a full 360 degrees, and a whole host of linked buildings: two cordite stores, ammunition store, a generator room and fuel store, a heating plant and ventilation room, officers command and sleeping quarters, NCO sleeping quarters, crew sleeping quarters, as well as a shower, toilet and washing facilities. Seventy-two men were working with each gun.

A myriad of other buildings were constructed too, most noticeable being the MP3 observation tower nearby! There was an underground command bunker and accommodation bunker, three ammunition stores, a water storage tank, mess hall and five different sets of searchlights. Then, of course, there were the additional defences in place to protect the big guns. A number of flak emplacements – one of which was altered in 1944 to allow a Wurzburg radar to be built on its base.

The range of the guns meant that it did see some action on D-Day – attacking naval units patrolling off of the Cotentin peninsula. After the war, the majority of the fixtures and fittings were removed, and today the battery is spread over private land, including that of a nearby school.

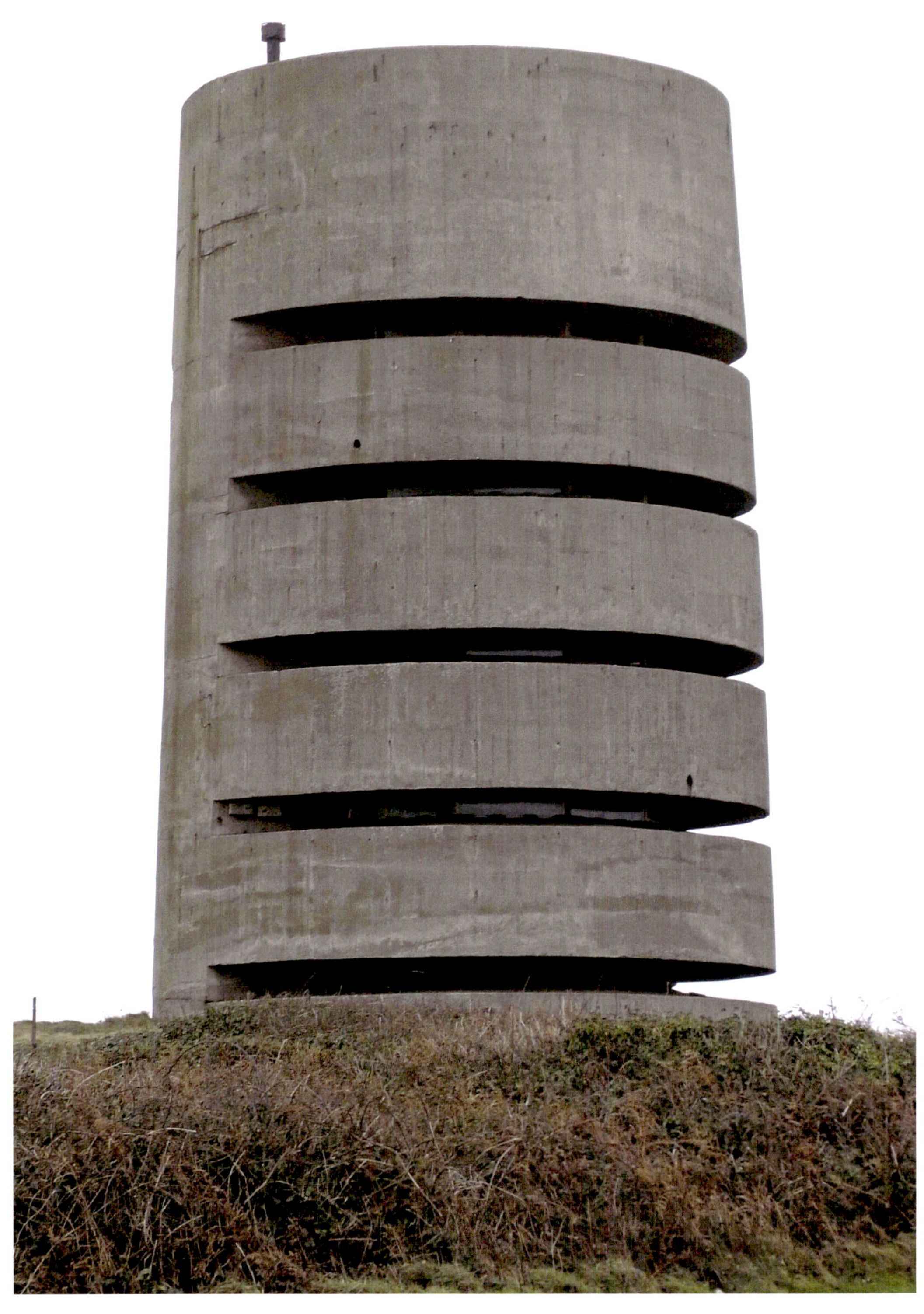

MP3 range-finding tower at Mirus Battery.

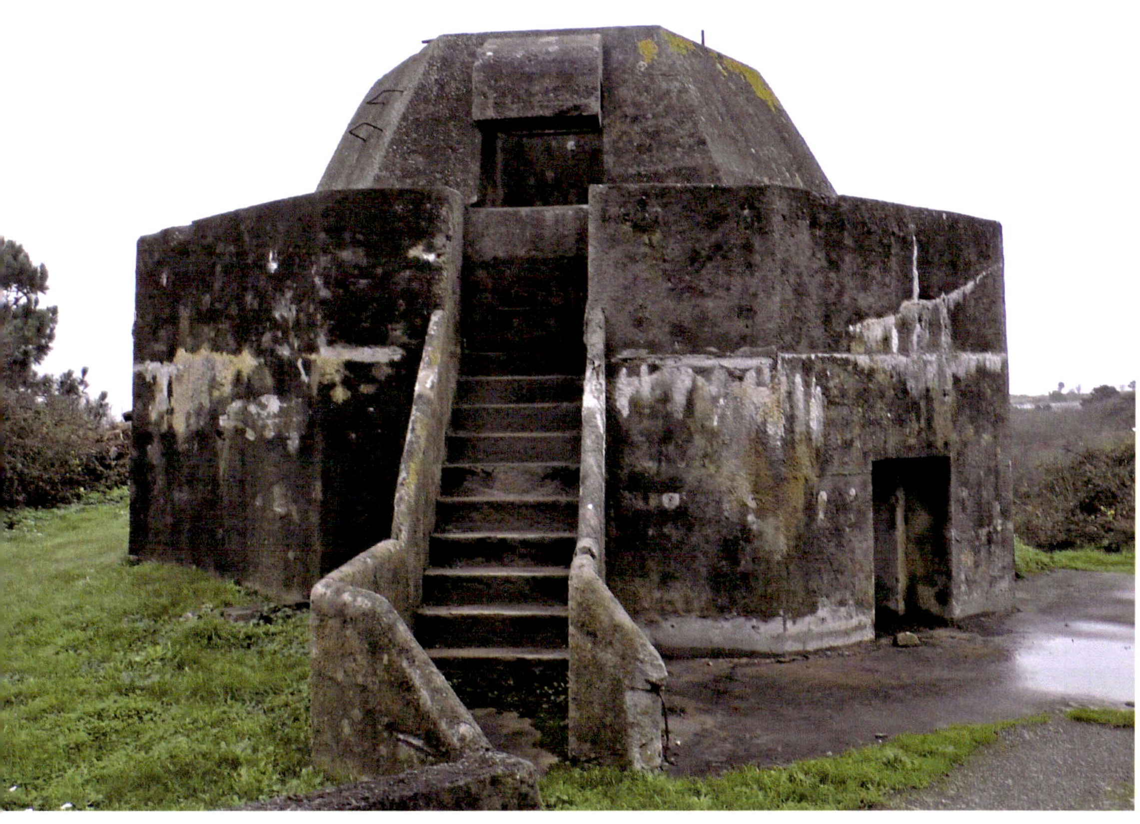

Originally an anti-aircraft position, the base was modified to take a radar antenna.

Pleinmont

The Pleinmont headland offers stunning views that extend for miles, so it is not surprising that all around there are a number of fortifications built from the German occupation during the Second World War. One fortification that stands out, literally, is the five-story naval observation tower that was built as part of their sea defence system during the occupation. Known as MP4, or L'Angle Tower, the fire control tower was designed to coordinate the fire from five different naval batteries on the island – with each level responsible for one of the batteries. Still with the original rangefinders onsite and in working order, inside there are maps of the Islands' military defences, as well as a mounted machine gun and field telephones. The roof offers a 360-degree view of the sea and surrounding countryside, as well as the nearby Battery Dollmann. With one of the four 22 cm gun pits and a number of trenches restored, it gives a glimpse at the original size of this battery. A command and observation bunker, accommodation and ammunition bunkers, along with barbed wire, flak positions, anti-tank guns and minefields made this a large site. Today, a French, 10-ton, 22 cm gun was restored by Guernsey Armouries in 1997 and sits in Gun Pit No. 3.

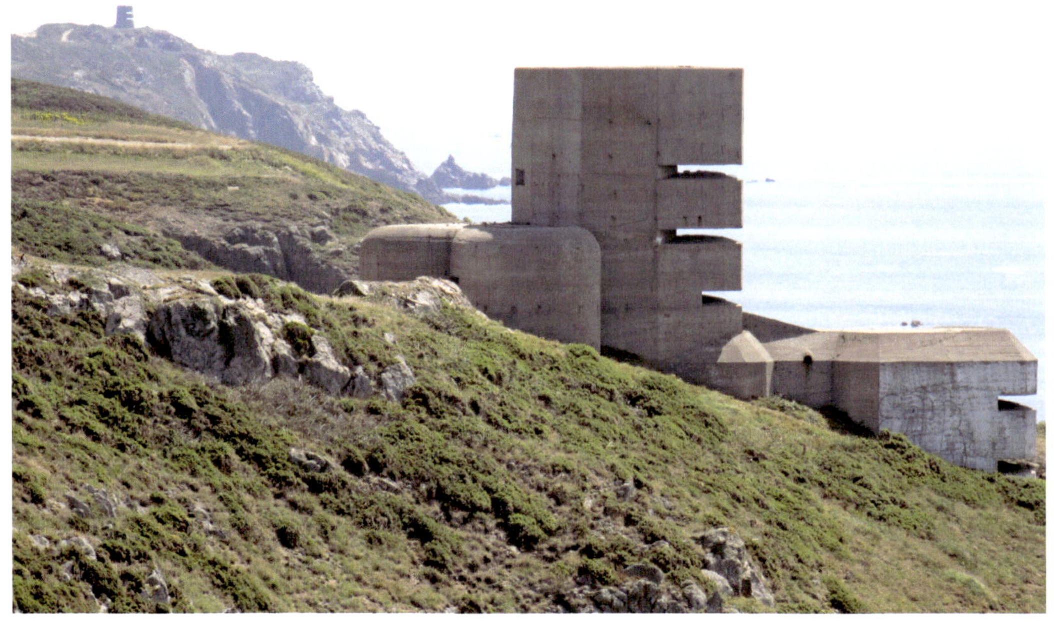

MP4 fire control tower on the Pleinmont headland. (Public domain)

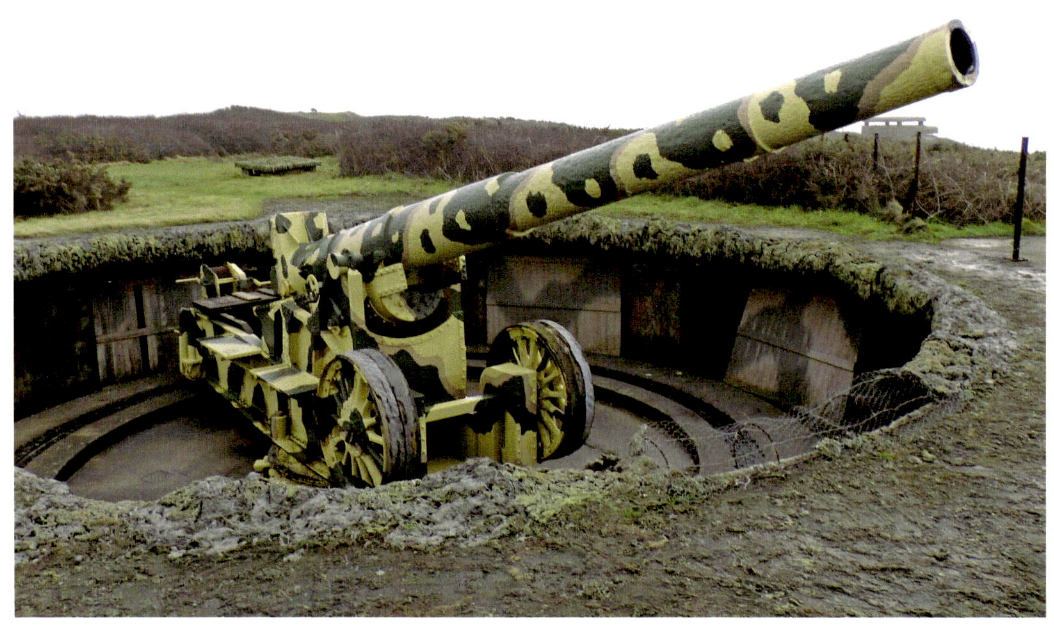

One of the gun pits at Battery Dollmann.

St Peter Port

It was in 1350 that King Edward III sent instructions to the Bailiff of Guernsey that he was to build a wall around the town. A large walled defensive position called Tour Beauregard was built in 1357 to command the southern and western approaches to the town. There is nothing left of this tower today as it was torn down in 1933 to allow for the widening of Cornet Street. During the Second World War, the headquarters of the German Naval Commander for the Channel Islands, was established next to La Collinette Hotel, and was responsible for all radio traffic to and from Germany and the other islands. You will also find La Valette Military Museum in St Peter Port – a museum dedicated to Guernsey's military history, specifically that of the German Occupation during the Second World War. The museum is actually set in a collection of air-conditioned tunnels that were built by German forces as a fuel storage facility for their U-boats – just one of some forty-one tunnel sites built between 1940 and 1945. The museum has a range of exhibitions, displays and information about the German occupation and the Guernsey Militia.

Steinbruch Battery

Built at the same time as Mirus Battery in 1941, Steinbruch Battery was constructed around the old quarry in Les Vardes, with four 15 cm naval guns in large open concrete positions. An ammunition bunker, personnel bunkers, anti-aircraft positions and a command bunker

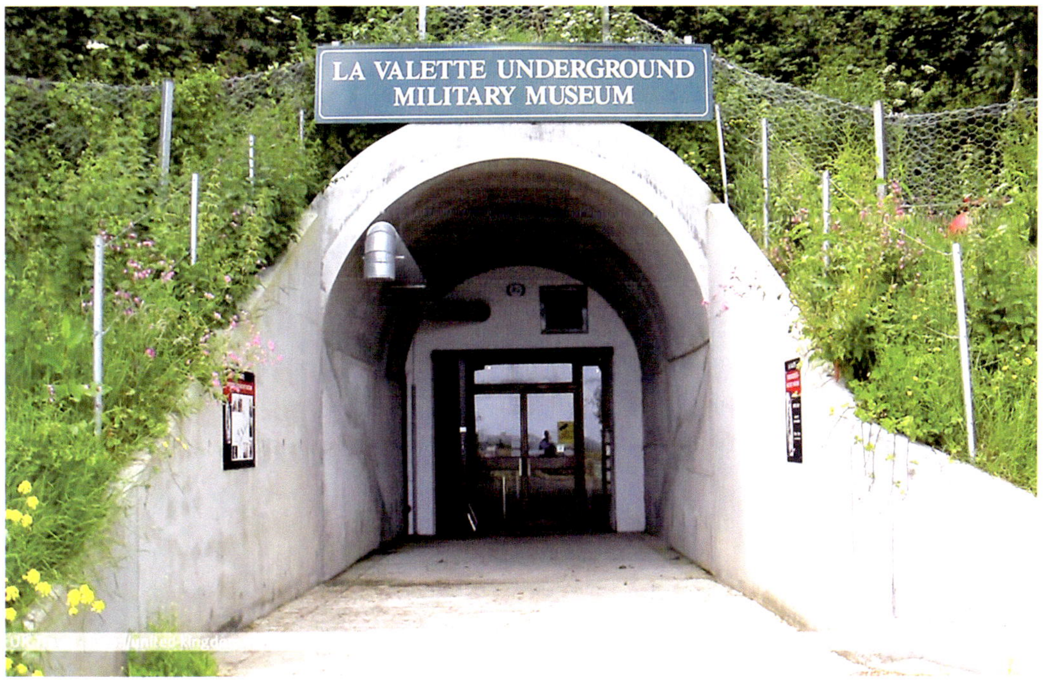

The entrance to La Valette Military Museum.

were all built on site. At the edge of the quarry, MP1 observation tower was built – one of the network of observation towers built around Guernsey designed to observe enemy ships and target their location for the batteries on the island to fire at. Sadly, due to the continued quarrying over the years, very little of the site remains.

Strassburg Battery

The third battery built by the Germans in 1941 was Strassburg, in the south-eastern corner of the island at Jerbourg Point. Like the others, it had four guns placed into large open concrete positions and these likely had a range of around 25 km. There was a large command bunker, ammunition and crew bunkers, various gun positions and two observation bunkers on the edge of the cliffs. In 1944, the Germans demolished the 'Doyle monument', which restricted the guns field of fire. Today, a lot of the site has been reclaimed by mother nature, although there are still some bunkers accessible.

Vale Castle

Originally called Le Chateau St Michel, the castle was first constructed on a hill around 1,000 years ago, to protect the local population against pirates. Overlooking St Sampson's harbour and Bordeaux Harbour, six towers, a curtain wall and a gatehouse were added in the fifteenth century, along with additional guardrooms and barrack accommodation for the garrison stationed there. During the English Civil War, it is likely that Parliamentarian troops may have been stationed in the now named Vale Castle. Towards the end of the eighteenth century, one 24-pounder and two 9-pounder cannons were added due to the threat of French invasion. During the Second World War, German occupying forces added a number of machine-gun positions, mortar positions, trenches and personnel shelters, along with two field guns and two searchlight positions. It is possible to visit these ruins all year round.

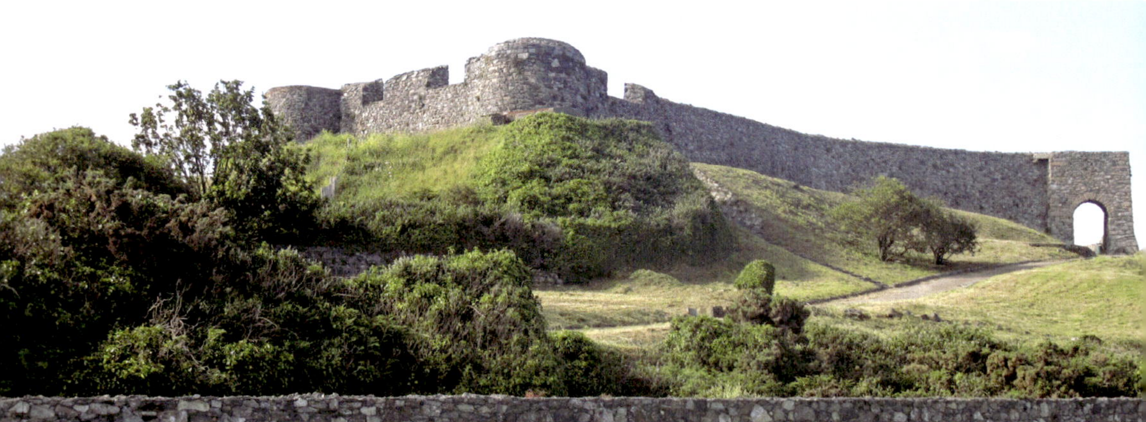

The impressive ruins of Vale Castle. (Public domain)

CHAPTER 3

Alderney

Alderney Militia

King Edward III authorised Thomas de Ferres to 'levy and train' militias in Jersey, Guernsey, Sark and Alderney in 1337, but very little by way of defensive structures were built, likely due to its smaller size, and it wasn't until 1657 that a Commander of the Militia was recorded. In the mid-eighteenth century, the militia numbered 200 men, and the French Revolution towards the end of that century saw 200 trained soldiers sent to Alderney. The loss of the thirty-eight-gun frigate HMS *Amethyst* in 1795 off the coast of Alderney provided the island with an opportunity to salvage what they could, with a number of cannons being recovered and used for the island's defences. By 1809, nineteen batteries had been built across the Alderney and these were manned by the over 350 men of the militia and the 500 plus soldiers now garrisoned here. By the mid-nineteenth century, the strength of the militia had reduced to around 150, but the now Royal Alderney Militia manned the fixed armaments at Fort Albert and Roselle Point. A number of men from the island served with 112 Company in France during the First World War, and in 1928 compulsory service was ended – the militia became a volunteer service. With the British government no longer bearing any cost with the militia, by the 1930s it was no more.

Battery Annes

Battery Annes was one of five batteries built by German forces in 1941. Located to the west of the island overlooking Les Casquets Lighthouse, it had four powerful 15 cm naval turreted guns in open emplacements. With a range of around fourteen miles, each of these had an attached ammunition store and crew bunker, with a central command post and additional storage areas. Searchlights and machine gun nests were dotted over the site, and just to the north, Flakbatterie Peil was armed with six 88 mm guns. Although the weapons have long since gone, the site is open to the public.

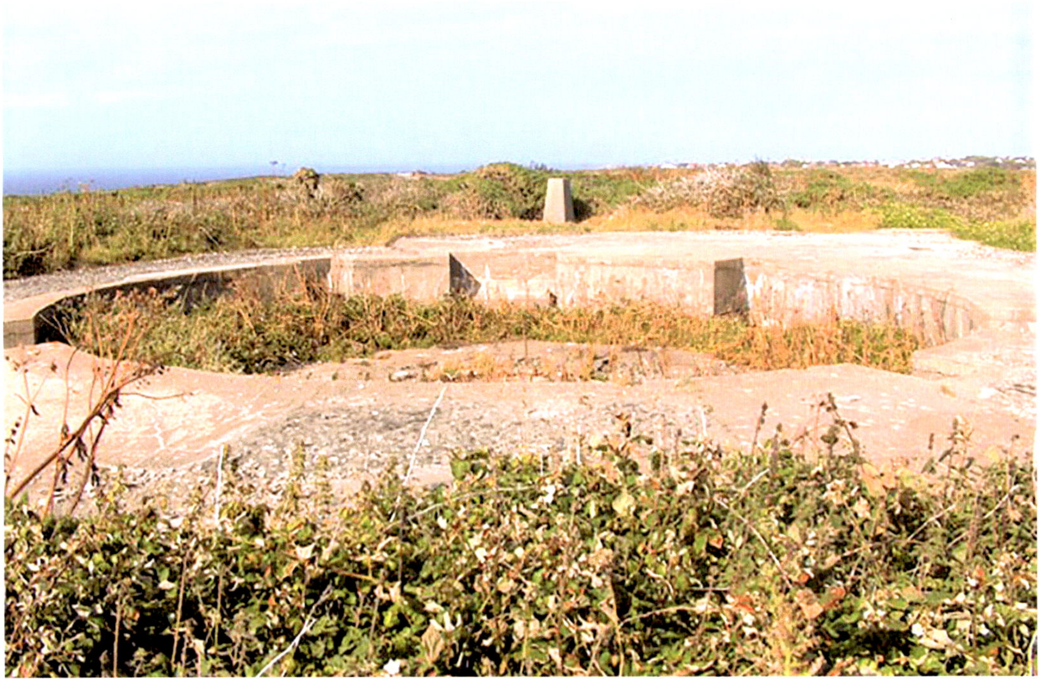

One of the gun emplacements at Battery Annes. (Courtesy of Ben Smitheon CC BY-SA 2.0)

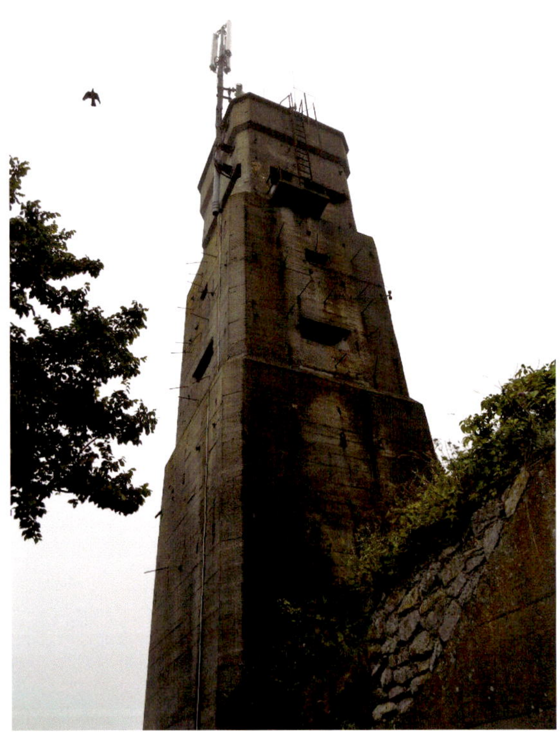

A German Luftwaffe observation tower at St Anne. (Courtesy of Ben Smitheon CC BY-SA 2.0)

Battery Blücher

Built during the German occupation in the centre of the island, there were four 15 cm K18 guns in open emplacements at this battery. With a fifteen-mile range, it is not surprising to know that in June 1944, Battery Blücher opened fire on American troops on the Cherbourg peninsula. The buildings associated with this battery no longer remain.

Battery Falke

Built in the middle of the island, not far from Battery Blücher, Battery Falke had four *Howitzers* in open field positions that could aim in any direction. Germany had captured a large number of First World War era guns when they conquered Poland, and later Hungary and Greece, and due to their age, they were incorporated into defensive lines and fortifications as opposed to front line use. Machine-gun nests and associated buildings were built here, but these are now long since gone.

Battery Marcks

Overlooking Braye Bay, German occupying forces took the remains of the Victorian era Roselle Battery, which originally had seven guns in it, and turned it into Battery Marcks. They installed four 10.5 cm cannons in concrete emplacements as a way of guarding the entrance to the only harbour on the island. Largely reclaimed by nature now, it is still possible to just make out the concrete bunkers, pillboxes and searchlight shelters.

Bibette Head

Not too far from Battery Marcks is Bibette Head. This was the German Strongpoint Biberkopf, which overlooks the sweeping sands of Saye Beach. This rocky peninsular had a 10.5 cm beach defence gun, as well as four anti-tank guns, machine-gun and mortar emplacements, along with trenches and tunnels.

Essex Castle

In 1546, work began on developing a fortification on the island, known as Essex Castle. Towers and walls were built with the aim of being able to garrison around two hundred men here. However, in 1554 work stopped, and the site was converted to a private residence for John Chamberlayne, the Lord of Alderney. In the 1840s the castle site was replaced by *Fort Essex*, a barracks for troops being garrisoned on the island, although some of the original walls remained, and today the ruins are a mixture of the two periods. German occupying forces did put two observation towers on to the fort.

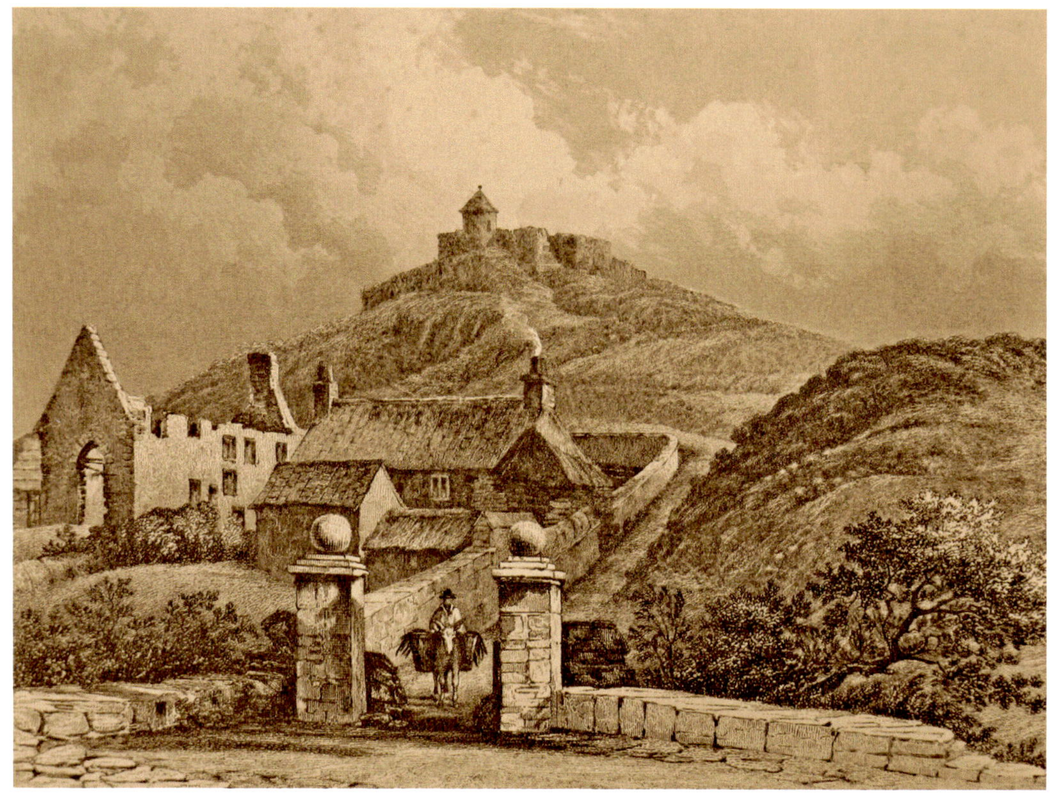

The Ruins of Essex Castle in the nineteenth century, Robert Mudie. (Public domain)

Fort Albert

Built in 1856 and originally called Fort Touraille, it was renamed after the death of Prince Albert in 1861. It was armed with an impressive arsenal of twenty-six 68-pounder guns and seventeen 8-inch guns. Overlooking the only harbour on the island, it was designed to be a strong coastal battery as well as the island's Citadel, and it was used as the military headquarters on Alderney until 1929. It is not surprising that during the German occupation, it became *Battery Elsass*, with three 17 cm guns installed here that had a range of 14 miles. Today, the site is closed to the public.

Fort Château à L'Etoc

Built in 1855 on a narrow headland, Fort Château à L'Etoc was built with the intention of providing protection for an eastern breakwater that was never actually built. Designed for a garrison of 128, it was armed with over twenty guns, with German forces occupying it during the Second World War. After the war it was redeveloped as private apartments.

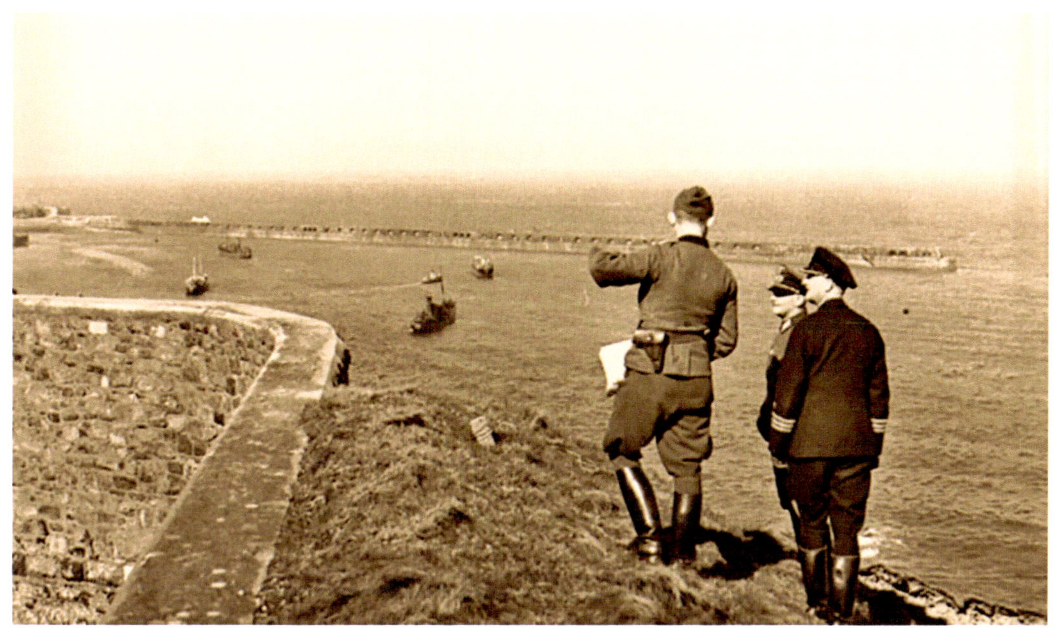

German forces inspecting the harbour from the walls of Fort Albert in 1942. (Courtesy of Bundesarchiv Bild 101II-MW-5152-14A CC BY-SA 3.0 DE)

Fort Clonque

Built on a small islet on the west of Alderney, Fort Clonque was constructed between 1847 – 1853 and is cut off from the rest of the island at high tide. Designed to protect the western approach to Alderney, it had ten guns and was manned by a crew of 50-60 soldiers. Like most Victorian Forts on the island, it was decommissioned in 1929, although the strategic position of it meant that German troops during the Second World War occupied it and added some more up-to-date gun positions. Today, it is managed by the Landmark Trust and it is possible to stay here!

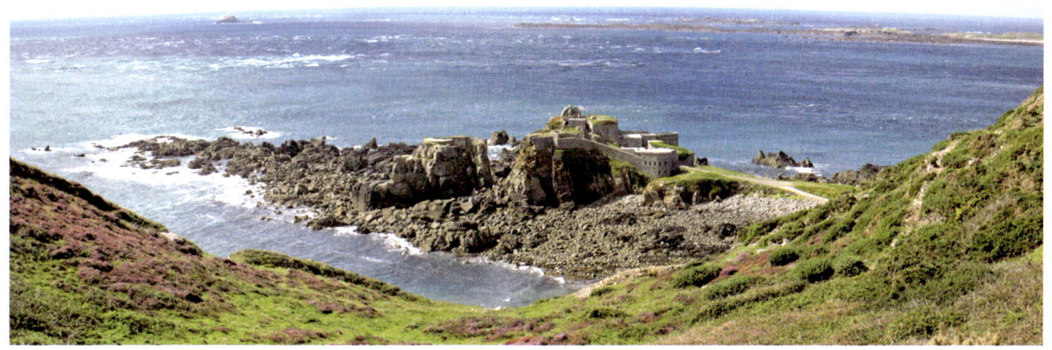

A view of Fort Clonque on the west of Alderney. (Courtesy of Andree Stephan CC BY 3.0)

Fort Corblets

Another Victorian era fort constructed in 1859, Fort Corblets was armed with five 32-pounder guns, three 24-pounders and five 8-inch guns that were housed in four batteries, with accommodation for sixty men. In the years after the Second World War, the fort received a partial redevelopment, and it is now used as a private residence.

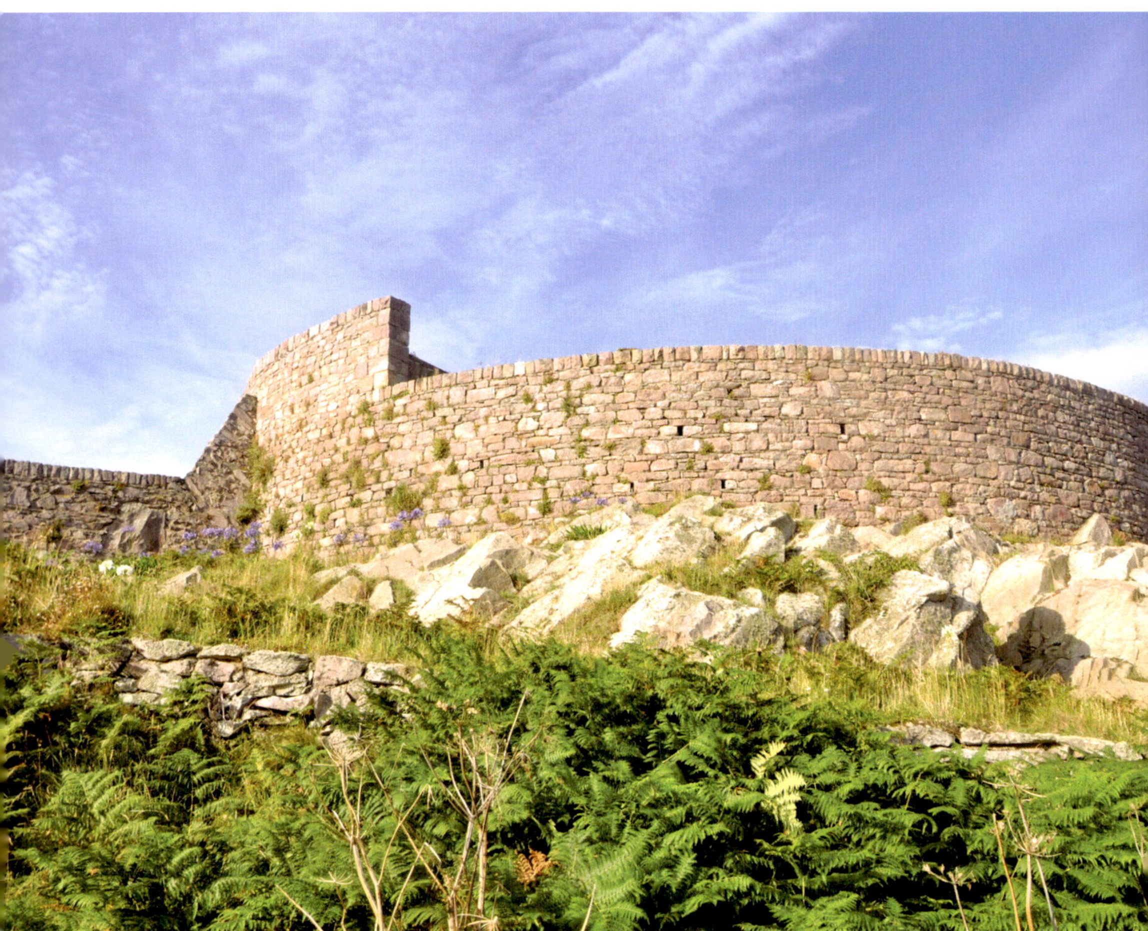

Fort Corblets is now available as a holiday let. (Courtesy of Richard James CC BY 2.0)

Fort Doyle

Fort Doyle was one of the earliest forts constructed on Alderney. Initially it had three 18-pounder cannons, which were then upgraded to an 8-inch howitzer and three 8-inch guns in 1859. German forces upgraded the fortifications in the area during the Second World War, with three coastal defence bunkers, mortar, anti-aircraft guns, machine-guns and trenches.

Fort Grosnez

Constructed between 1851 and 1853, Fort Grosnez was built at the western end of the breakwater which protects the only harbour on the island. Located at the end of the longest breakwater in the country, it is not surprising that that is had an impressive arsenal of two 8 inch howitzers, six 68-pounder guns, sixteen 32-pounders, and four 24-pounders! During the German occupation an anti-aircraft Battery was installed here.

Fort Houmet Herbe

Another of Alderney's Victorian era forts constructed to protect the island from potential French attack, Fort Houmet Herbe was built on a small island on the north-east which is cut off by the high tide. In 1859, it was armed with one 8-inch howitzer and nine 8-inch guns. Although the outer walls remain, sadly, it has been left derelict for a long time.

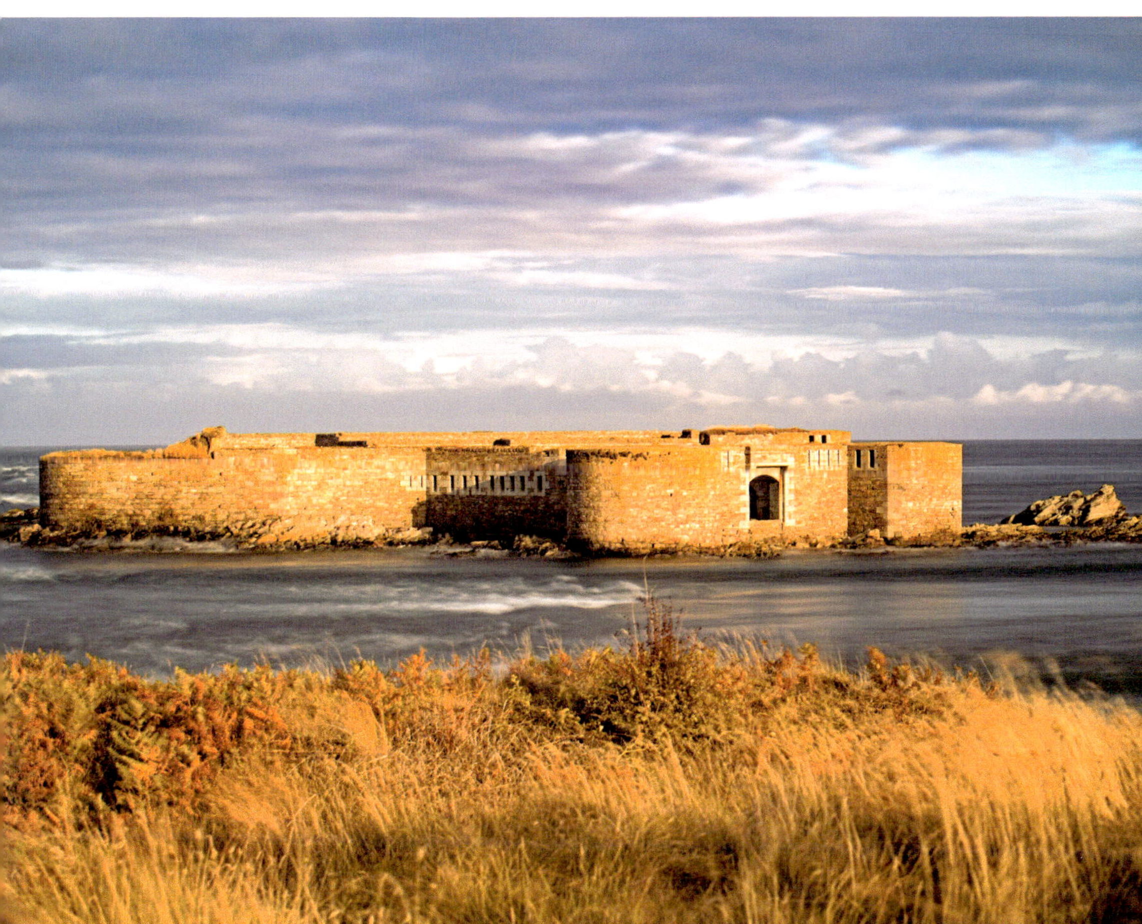

A stunning view of Fort Houmet Herbe. (Courtesy of Richard James CC BY-ND 2.0)

Fort Ile de Raz

Built in the 1850s, Fort Ile de Raz sits on a small tidal island in Longis Bay, which is just off the north-east coast of Alderney. Situated less than a mile south from Fort Houme Herbé, it has a 400-metre causeway leading to it at low tide and was garrisoned by around sixty men and ten guns. The Germans occupied the site during the Second World War but it now sits derelict with no public access.

Fort Les Hommeaux Florains

Built in 1859 on a small island protecting Cat's Bay, Fort Les Hommeaux Florains was armed with three 68-pounder guns, and four 32-pounders with barrack accommodation for nearly seventy men. This fort is now sits in ruins.

Fort Tourgis

Completed 1855, Fort Tourgis was designed to be Alderney's largest fort with a garrison of nearly 350 men! By 1859, it was armed with eight 68-pounder guns, ten 32-pounders and fifteen 8-inch guns and four 13-inch mortars. German forces used the fort during the occupation, and it was still in use for a short time after the Second World War by the army. In recent years, a lot of work has taken place in clearing and conserving the site, with Cambridge Battery and Battery No. 3 open to the public.

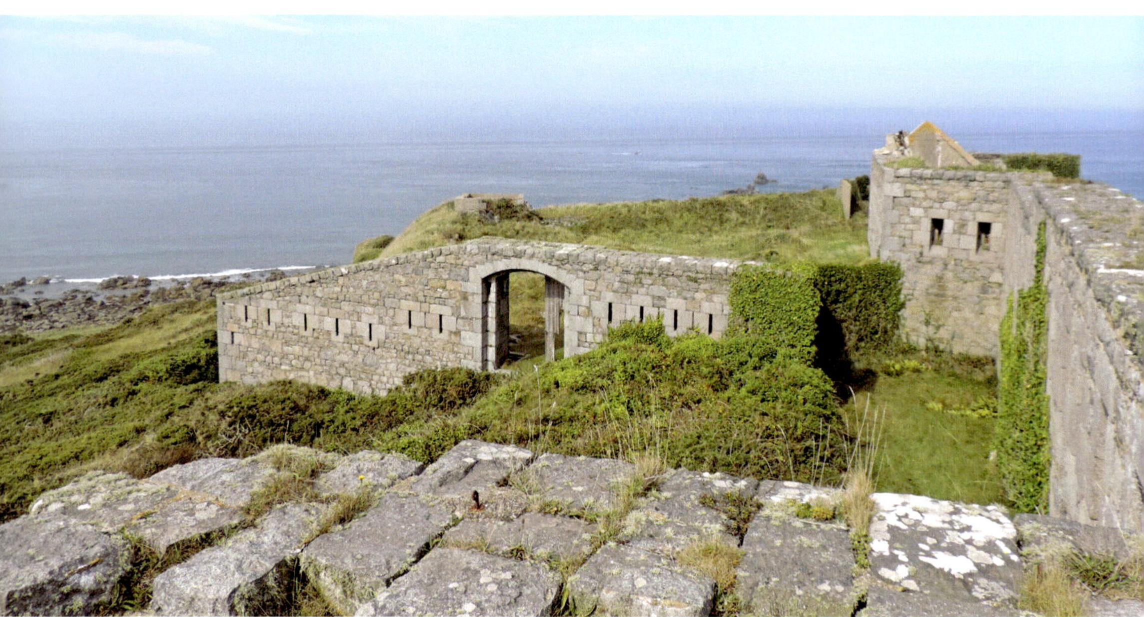

Fort Tourgis. (Courtesy of Daniel Kraft CC BY-SA 3.0)

Fort Quesnard

Built in 1859, Fort Quesnard was armed with three 32-pounder guns, four 8-inch guns and was manned by 55 soldiers. The fort is now used as a private residence.

German Camps

During the occupation of the Second World War, German forces built four camps on Alderney. They were set up under the Organisation Todt (OT) in 1942, although some were later run by the notorious Schutzstaffel – better known as the SS.

Lager Borkum was the smallest of the four camps and was situated near the centre of Alderney. It was able to hold several hundred people, and although few records survive of the conditions, it is thought that this camp was occupied by OT staff and personnel from conscripted European construction companies. They would have been directly involved in the construction of bunkers on the island, and as such, conditions were likely not as bad as in the other camps. This was the only camp to remain after liberation in 1945 as it was briefly used as a military barracks. Today, two sets of masonry gateposts on the camp perimeter survive.

Lager Helgoland covered quite a large area of land at Platte Saline and could hold around 1,500 inmates. Russian prisoners of war, Ukrainian and Polish forced labourers, as well as Jews from occupied Europe, worked twelve-hour days, seven days a week, with minimal food rations and very poor conditions. They were essentially slave labour for the numerous building projects taking place. The Germans began dismantling the camp as early as the winter of 1943, and the vast majority of the site, aside from the gateposts, has been built over with new housing developments.

Lager Norderney in the north-east of the island held up to 1,500 workers and started out as a *'typical'* OT labour camp – with inmates being used to build the concrete defences on the island. Forced labour from German occupied countries was brought in to keep the quota of workers required, but things changed somewhat when over 550 French Jews were brought over in 1943 by the notorious SS. The Jewish prisoners were kept in a separate wired-off part of the camp and were likely treated in an awful way. Little remains of this camp, although the former Saye farmhouse, which was used as the OT commandant's quarters, still exists.

Lager Sylt in the south-west of Alderney was originally run by the Organisation Todt (OT), but in early 1943, SS Construction Brigade I arrived in Alderney with over 900 prisoners from the Sachsenhausen concentration camp near Berlin. The SS enlarged the site in order to accommodate more prisoners and it is probable that conditions here were inhumane during their fifteen months in charge. The SS withdrew from the camp with around 650 prisoners back to mainland Europe in the summer of 1944, when it was clear the D-Day landings had been a success. The German troops left on the island demolished and burned much of the camp to the ground, along with any records associated with their use, before the island was liberated by British forces – and it is interesting to note that the Alderney garrison did not surrender until a week after the other Channel Islands on 16 May 1945.

It had been estimated that over 700 people died in the Alderney camps.

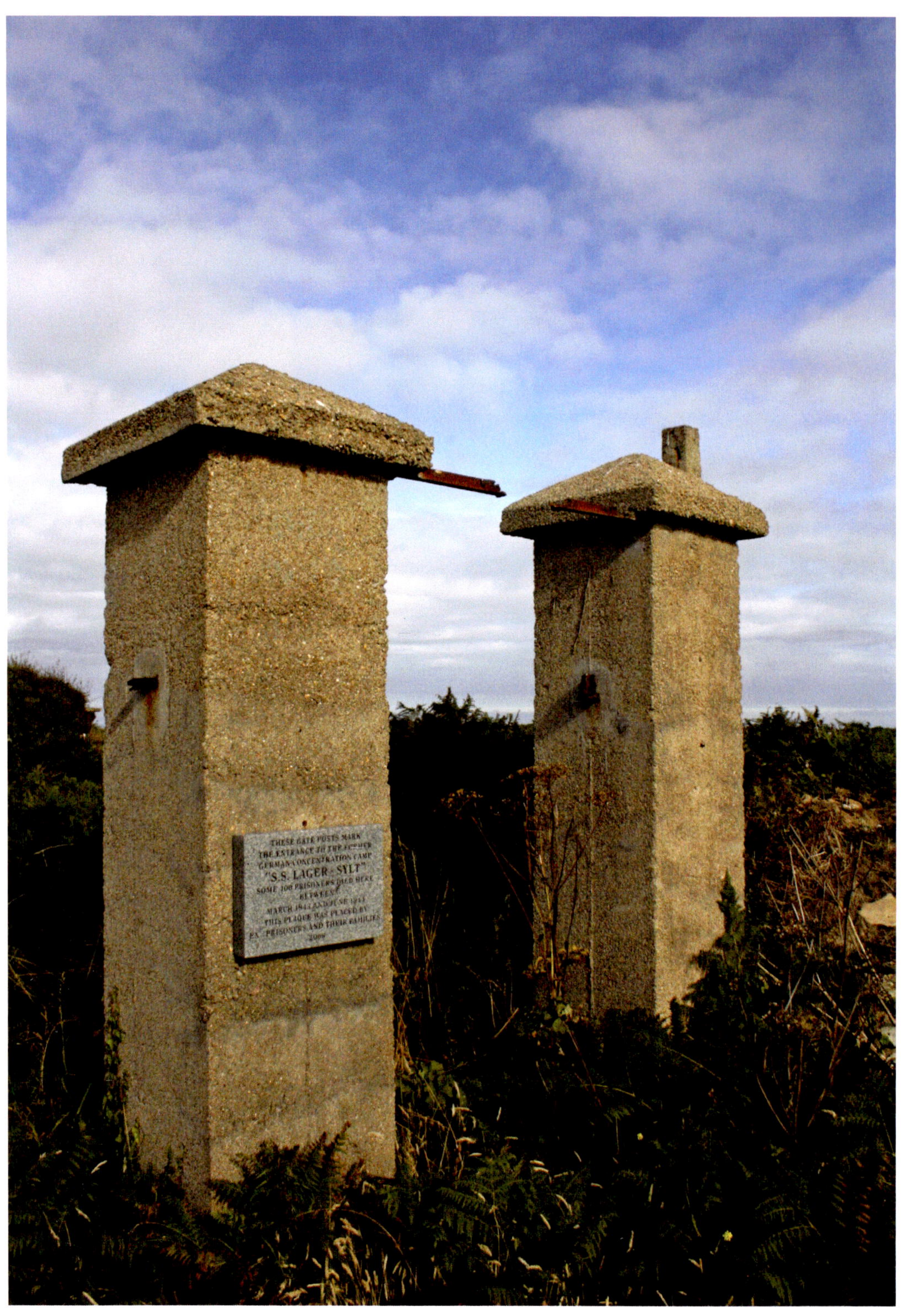

The gateposts to Lager Sylt. (Courtesy of The Only Moxey CC BY 2.0)

Longis Bay

Longis Bay, on the south-east coast of the island, has a half-mile-long sandy beach which is the longest stretch of sand in Alderney. At low tide, the water retreats over a mile, so during the German occupation, they were fearful that this could be used as a possible landing site to liberate the island. As a result, they built a long anti-tank wall, which still stands today.

Marinepeilstand 3

Built in 1943, MP3 is a massive concrete tower that was to be used as a Naval range-finder. This was to be one of six on the island, although the others were never built. The rounded front section was for observation with each level linked to one of the island's three coastal gun batteries at Annes, Blücher and Elsass. Today it is open to the public and known as The Odeon.

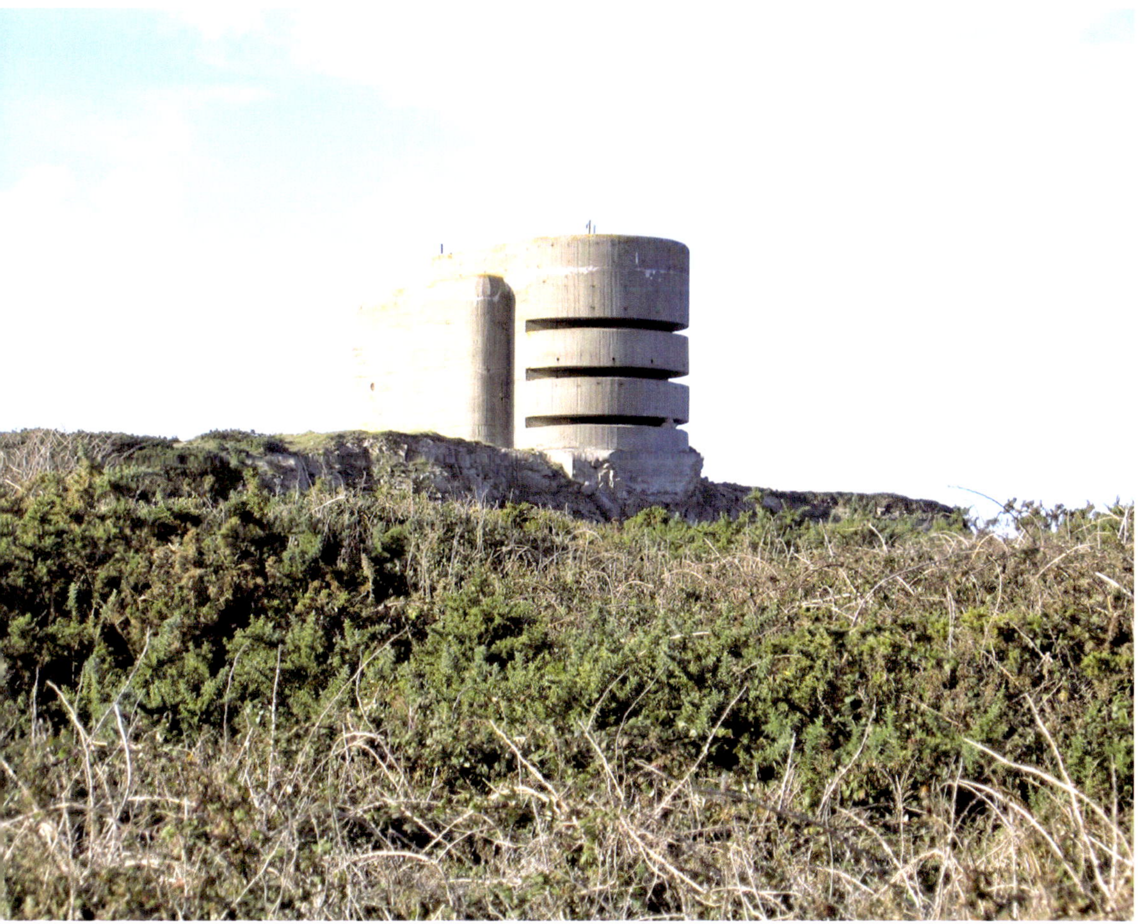

The Odeon. (Courtesy of Tim Brighton CC BY-SA 2.0)

CHAPTER 4

Sark and Herm

Sark

The small island of Sark did have its own militia, which began 1565, as a result of the French military occupying the island from 1549 to 1553. The French built three forts, which the liberating Guernsey Militia tore down, but the wall and bastion of a fourth fort along the spine of L'Eperquerie was kept and repaired to be used to defend the island in the future. During the English Civil War of the 1640s, Sark's royalist Seigneur joined Jersey in showing allegiance to the Crown, whilst Guernsey favoured the Parliamentarians, and as a result, Guernsey Parliamentarian militia men were billeted on Sark families! After this, every man aged between 16 and 60 had to serve with the island's militia, and in 1793 cannons were sent to Sark to bolster defences – many of which remain there today. The Sark Militia were disbanded at the end of the nineteenth century.

During the Second World War, Sark was occupied by German forces. Sibyl Hathaway, the Seigneur of Sark, encouraged the islanders to remain and not evacuate – with the huge majority following her wishes. When the Germans arrived, she tried to manipulate situations that would result in favourable terms for Sark and its population. She spoke German and infamously expected officers to bow to her and kiss her hand! The German troops established some minefields on the beaches and cliffs; and installed some anti-aircraft guns and an anti-tank gun in 1943. It wasn't until 1944 that some sort of fortification was built, with three 8.8 cm guns from a sunken ship being placed in *Battery Klein Sark*. During the five years of occupation, there were some small British Commando raids to the island and there are some graves of men who lost their lives during these.

Herm

German forces claimed Herm on 20 July 1940, and used the beaches of Herm to practise landings in preparation for a potential invasion of England, under the guise of shooting a propaganda film titled *The Invasion of the Isle of Wight*. Aside from a small mobile anti-aircraft battery being placed on the island for a short space of time, no other fortifications were built.

About the Author

Andrew Powell-Thomas writes military history, local heritage, and children's fiction books. He regularly speaks at events, libraries, schools and literary festivals, as well as making appearances on television and radio. It is possible to keep up with everything he is up to by following him on social media or by visiting his website at www.andrewpowell-thomas.co.uk.

Andrew's other titles available from Amberley Publishing:

The West Country's Last Line of Defence: Taunton Stop Line
Historic England: Somerset
50 Gems of Somerset
50 Gems of Wiltshire
50 Gems of Jersey
50 Gems of the Isle of Wight
Cornwall's Military Heritage
Devon's Military Heritage
Somerset's Military Heritage
Wiltshire's Military Heritage
The Isle of Wight's Military Heritage
Castles and Fortifications of the West Country
Castles of Scotland

Acknowledgements

What a fascinating book this has been to research. I have been fortunate enough to have visited the Channel Islands a number of times on holiday in my life, and each time I have discovered more incredible places of history, which have simply made me want to return again and again. This book has been an exhilarating and time-consuming process. I've been able to rediscover locations, buildings and ruins, in addition to uncovering numerous new sights, sounds and stories. The Channel Islands have layer upon layer of history and unravelling this, and attempting to condense so much heritage into just one book, was a challenge to say the least! In this day in age it is possible to do a lot of research online, but nothing compares to actually heading out and exploring things for yourself, which I have had great delight in doing. Only then, when you see these stunning and historic locations in their original environment, does it start to make sense and your writing can take shape. Investigating the different aspects of this book has led me to find out some incredible things and meet a number of wonderful people and organisations, all of whom have been willing to share their knowledge and expertise, and this is so important in passing on the history of our communities to the next generation.

I need to express my gratitude to the many organisations, people and photographers who have kindly shared their knowledge, offered me support and allowed me to use their photographic work in my book: Dave Sewell, Damien Horn from the Channel Islands Military Museum and everyone at the Channel Islands Occupation Society (CIOS) for their warmth, knowledge and enthusiasm, especially Daniel Clark and Malcolm Amy. There also needs to be a mention for everyone at Jersey Heritage, especially Hilary Grimes, Val Nelson and Helena Kergozou, who have been so helpful and accommodating across all their sites, as well as being willing to share their expertise with me.

I would also like to thank Nick Grant, Nikki Embery, Jenny Bennett and all at Amberley Publishing for their help in making this project become a reality, as well as my wife, Laura, and sons, James and Ryan, who accompanied me on some wonderful trips to these beautiful islands, and who can't wait to return and explore again.